THE
SAILING SHIPS
OF
ALN & COQUET

Front cover
Barque *Meggie Dixon* of Amble.
Capt. I.C. Mann 20th April 1873
Oil painting by J. Hudson (1829-c1896)
Original can been viewed in the
Trinity Maritime Centre, 29, Broad Chare,
Quayside, Newcastle upon Tyne.
(Courtesy: Mr F. Mann)

The Sailing Ships
of
Aln & Coquet

A record of the sailing ships
of the Rivers Aln and Coquet
from
1830 to 1896

by

Richard E. Keys

Richard E. Keys
1993

i

ISBN 0 - 9521275 - 0 - 4

Published by Richard E. Keys,
99, St John's Road,
Newcastle upon Tyne,
NE4 7TJ
(091) 2260965

Printed in Great Britain by
Tyneside Free Press,
5, Charlotte Square,
Newcastle upon Tyne,
NE1 4XF

Preface

In the mid-nineteen sixties, I spent an enjoyable summer cruising the Northumbrian Coast aboard the yachts *Billy Bud* and *Loafer*. Frequent visits were made to the Rivers Aln and Coquet and their ports, Alnmouth and Amble (or Warkworth Harbour, to give its official name). Alnmouth put one in mind of a select Victorian watering place, while Amble, with its staiths still standing, had the visage of a coal port. Places of marked contrasts, and very different histories, the names Alnmouth and Amble became imprinted on my memory.

A couple of decades were to pass before those names consciously re-entered my mind. It occurred when I was working on a history of the Tyne's sailing ships. As I trawled through countless newspaper files, Custom House Registers, and the like, it soon became apparent that the Aln and Coquet, had also been home to a fleet of merchant sailing ships. Although their numbers were tiny compared with the vast fleets emanating from Port of Tyne, Blyth, or Sunderland, they played a small but significant role in the commercial activities of the area. The smaller ships, for the most part, carried away agricultural products from Alnmouth and coal from Amble. When a return cargo could be procured, they brought home pit props, timber and building materials. It is doubtful if some of the larger ships owned in the area ever entered their home ports. Some, such as the 586 ton *Manfred* belonging to William Davison of Alnwick, was to large to risk crossing the bar of the Aln. Ships of her ilk spent their days wandering the globe earning a living by picking up whatever cargoes came their way. They were more likely to be encountered in the ports of the Dutch East Indies (now Indonesia) than those of mid-Northumberland! It was a phenomena shared by a number of United Kingdom ports in the days when Britain had the largest merchant fleet in the world.

Like most of the sailing ships belonging to other North-East rivers, those of the Aln and Coquet had disappeared by the end of the Nineteenth Century. None survived long enough to become targets for preservation. When their end came they were regarded as maritime junk in a world awash with obsolete windjammers. Little was left to mark their passing.

Acknowledgements

I am most grateful to the many people who have helped in the compilation of this work. In particular I would like to thank Dr Tony Barrow, M.Ed., Ph.D., for reading the manuscript, giving advice and putting me on the scent of a number of illustrations; Dennis Nicholson for generously making his work on the Berwick Ship Registers available; Graeme H. Somner, Harold S. Appleyard, Keith O'Donoghue and Philip Thomas, of the World Ship Society, Central Record Team, for valuable contributions to the *Fleet List* and *Appendix II*; Major R.P. Rising, R.M., Secretary of the Royal Yacht Squadron, for information about the Hugh Andrews steam yachts; Ian Rae for his notes on the Wigham Richardson and C.S. Swan built steamers; John Dobson and Ron French, who gave encouragement and the benefit of their specialist knowledge.

Thanks also to the staff of the following institutions for their unfailing help and courtesy:

Newcastle City Library.
Morpeth Library.
South Shields Library.
Tyne and Wear Archives Service.
Northumberland Record Office.
Cleveland Archives.

Last, but by no means least, thanks to my long suffering family, past and present, who have put up with my obsession with ships and the sea for so many years.

Illustrations

Contents

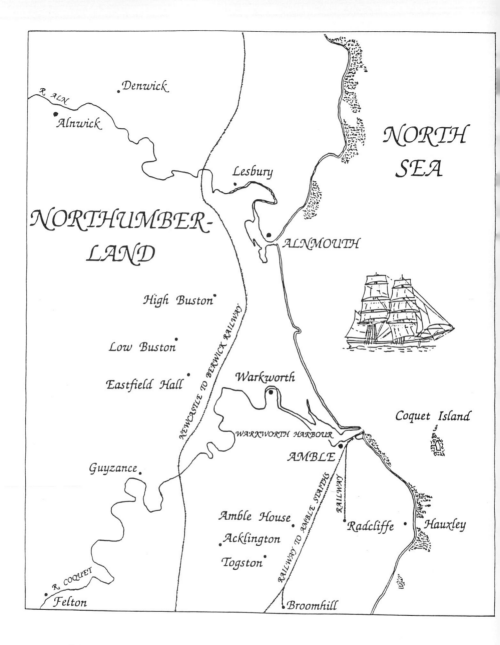

Map of mid-Northumberland showing where the Owners and Shareholders of the
Aln and Coquet sailing ships resided.
(Map by R.E. Keys)

1

The
Sailing Ships
of
Aln & Coquet

This is an account of the small fleet of merchant sailing ships belonging to the towns and villages situated near the lower reaches of the Northumbrian rivers Aln and Coquet. It begins in the 1830's when an Act of Parliament laid the foundation for the creation of Warkworth Harbour at the entrance to the Coquet.

Over 170 sailing ships were owned in the area which is now administered by Alnwick District Council. They ranged in size from the tiny twenty-six ton, Amble built schooner *Luck's All* to the 946 ton barque *Camperdown* belonging to Hugh Andrews, the wealthy coal owner and proprietor of Warkworth Harbour. Two hundred and fifty-three tons larger than any other locally owned vessel, the *Camperdown* was an anomaly. The average Aln/Coquet owned vessel measured about 200 registered tons, had a length of 96 feet, breadth of 24 feet, and could carry about 350 tons of cargo.

Trades

A glance at the *Fleet List,* included in this book, reveals where the Aln and Coquet vessels voyaged to - northward to Archangel, eastward into the Baltic. Southward into the Mediterranean and Black Seas, still further eastward, around the Cape of Good Hope, to the coasts of China, Java, Burma, and India; westward to the West Indies, North and South America. But, the most frequent of all, were coastwise voyages and short hauls to near Continental ports.

Coal was their main outward cargo, loaded at Amble, on the Tyne, Wear, and at Blyth. The rise of Amble as a seaport coincided with an increased demand for the commodity. Industry needed it for power and manufacturing processes both at home and abroad, municipalities for gas lighting; railways and steamships were impotent without it. Coal depots were established along the world's trade routes to re-fuel the growing numbers of steamers. They had to be regularly replenished. All these requirements provided work for the sailing ship.

2

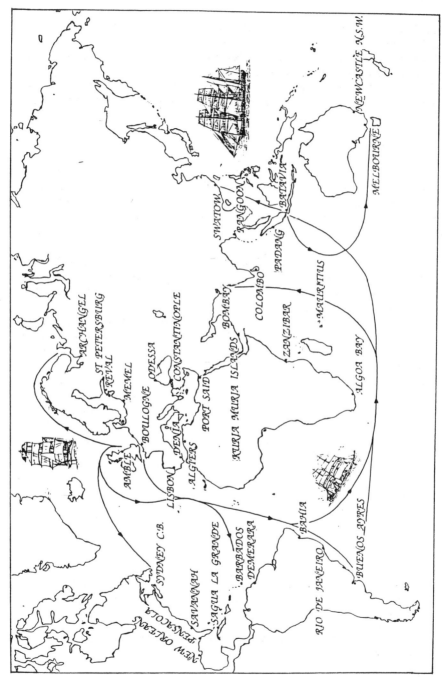

Map of the World showing some of the places known to have been visited by Aln and Coquet sailing ships and the outward bound routes they would have probably followed.

(Map by R F Keys)

3

Once they had reached their destinations and discharged, the deep water ships usually went "tramping" picking up whatever profitable freight presented itself. In 1886, after discharging coal at Trinidad, Hugh Andrews brig *Hiawatha* went to Mobile, Alabama, where she was lucky enough to get a cargo of logs for Amble; by contrast the barque *Campsie Glen,* belonging to the Davison family of Alnwick, made calls at ports in North America, Burma, Java, Argentina, Australia and New Zealand in the course of one long voyage in the years 1881/82.

A Passage in the Coal Trade

No log or description of a voyage in the London coal trade, aboard an Aln or Coquet vessel, has been found locally but the log of the Newcastle schooner *Sally*, which made a passage from the Tyne to London in 1845, still survives. Built at Sunderland in 1838, the *Sally* measured 135 tons. She was similar in rig and size to the Alnmouth schooner *Prospect* and the Amble owned *Seaflower,* both built on the Wear in 1846 and 1849 respectively.

The *Sally* could carry about 80 chaldrons (212 tons) of coal. In most North-East ports the colliers loaded at staiths. These were massive wooden structures which carried the coal laden railway wagons out to a point in the river where the water was sufficiently deep for a vessel to get alongside. The coal was transferred to the colliers hold by drops or spouts. By the drop method the wagon was lowered down to near deck level before being emptied into the hold. The spout was basically a shoot leading from the staith to the hold. Coal was dropped through the bottom of a wagon into the spout.

At six o'clock on the evening of 10 June 1845 the *Sally* left the "spouts" (her log does not indicate where exactly these were) and was towed out to sea by the steam tug *Collingwood,* just one of 212 colliers to leave the Tyne that week. Two and a half hours later the tug was discharged: "made all sail; light winds West. At 5 a.m. in studding sails; light wind S.S.E." The log continues:

> *June 11th.* The whole of these 24 hours fine pleasant weather with light winds at S. by E. ship flying to windward.
> *June 12th.* The whole of these 24 hours fine and pleasant weather with light winds and variable. Midnight Flambrough Head Light bearing south.
> *June 13th.* These 24 hours light airs with calms at intervals. Midnight Flambro Head Light bearing N.W.
> *June 14th.* Commenced light airs E.N.E. set the studding sails. At 6 p.m. thick foggy weather; more clear at 8 p.m. Foggy weather.
> *June 15th.* Commenced foggy and calm. At 2 a.m. more clear; set fore topmast studding sail. Light air E by N. At 8 a.m. in studding sail. Wind S.E. Dudgeon Light bearing S.E. by S. Tacked ship to the eastwards. At 4 p.m. tacked ship to the S.S.W. Midnight light winds S.S.E.
> *June 16th.* Commenced light winds S.S.E. ship plying to windward. At 4 p.m. came to anchor in 10 fathoms water. Low water. Got under weigh; flying to windward.

4

June 17th. Commenced light wind South. Ship flying to wind ward. Came to anchor off Cromer in 8 fathoms. Low water underweigh.
June 18th. Commenced light wind variable. At 8 p.m. came to anchor in the Cockle gatt (off Winterton). Midnight light wind E.S.E.
June 19th. Commenced light wind S.E. At 3 a.m. got underweigh proceeded through roads (Yarmouth Roads). At 7 a.m. came to an anchor in Lowestoft Roads. Thick foggy weather. Low water got underweigh. Wind variable. At 11 p.m. came to anchor in 7 fathoms. Wind N.W. light winds.
June 20th. At 3 a.m. got underweigh. Winds variable from W.N.W. to S.S.E. Midnight. came to anchor in sea reach. Low water got under weigh. wind E.S.E. proceeded up the river (Thames)."

The *Sally's* passage from the Tyne to London had taken a little over ten days. Her log does not commence again until 7 July when she sailed out from the Tyne bound for the Rhone with another cargo of coal. It would be reasonable to assume that she had arrived back in the river early in July having made the voyage to and from London in about 20 days.

The Alnmouth brig *Marquis of Wellington* (Capt. Gibb) was probably in the Thames with the *Sally*. She had left Amble at about the same time as the *Sally* had left the Tyne. The *Marquis* earned a freight of 8/-(40p) per ton.

A glance at the *Shipping Intelligence* columns of the summer of 1845, when the *Sally* was making her London voyage, gives a good insight into what the Aln/Coquet coasters were up to.

Movements in Months of June/July, 1845:

From Amble:- Sloop *Trader* (Capt. James Straker) to Alnmouth with guano; Schooner *Lady Nepean* (Capt. Henry Heatley) to Hull; Brig *Earl of Newburgh* (Capt. George Liddle) and *Marquis of Wellington* (after her London voyage), both to Honfleur with coal. It is interesting to note that a vessel called the *Mary* (Capt. Douglas) took coal to Waren, in Budle Bay.

To Amble:- Schooner *Express* (Capt. Gibb) from Alnmouth in ballast; Sloop *Trader* (Capt. James Straker) from Craister with limestone.

From Newcastle:- Schooner *Alnwick Castle* (Capt. George Potter) to Alnmouth with "goods."

Record Voyage of the *Friends Goodwill*

The *Newcastle Journal* of 17 October 1846 described a voyage made by the Ipswich registered schooner *Friends Goodwill* (Capt. Jackson) as: "the most expeditious voyage that has been made to this port (Amble) . . . from London." This 63 ton ship had left the north on 1 October. Three days had been spent discharging at London from where the northward run to Amble had taken only 39 hours. The *Journal* also reported that her master intended taking up residence in Warkworth.

The quaintly named *Friends Goodwill* was an interesting old timer. Originally called *Gauilda Maria,* she had been condemned as a prize by the High Court of Admiralty on 7 July 1812 after being captured by H.M. Sloop-of-War *Calypso*. She became North-East Coast owned during 1852 when William Boutland, a Bill Quay shipbuilder, acquired her. She went missing after leaving the Tyne for London on 1 November 1861

Discharging Coal at London

It was the usual practice for an incoming collier to come to moorings off Gravesend. From there the master sent his ship's papers up to a factor at the coal exchange, informing him of the quality and quantity of the coal he had. When the coal was sold, orders would be given by the harbour master to proceed up to the Pool, a mile long stretch of river between Ratcliff-cross and Execution Dock, to discharge. The Pool of those days must have been a lively place. Sometimes a fleet of two to three hundred colliers would congregate there. Here is a description of how the mooring of all these vessels was arranged just a few years before steam arrived on the scene:

> "The Pool is divided into the Upper and Lower Pool; the Lower consists of seven tiers, which generally contain each from fourteen to twenty ships; these are moored stern to stern and lie from seven to ten abreast. The Upper Pool contains about ten tiers. The four tiers at Mill-hole are equally large with the tiers of the Lower Pool."[1]

The colliers were assisted on their way upstream by watermen, usually belonging to Greenwich, who were very skilled at handling craft in the very crowded waterway. The berthing was done without aid of steam tugs. Working the sails and braces, the collier's way would be checked just as she reached the mooring buoy. Then: "the youngest man on board would jump on to the buoy with a handy rope, catch a turn, and make fast another rope at once, and then we would furl the sails."[2] If they made a mess of the manoeuvre the anchor had to be let go, sails furled, and a warp run out to the buoy so that the collier could be hauled near and moored securely.

Discharging the coal was done by gangs of "coal-whippers" - a gang consisting of nine men. Four of these were employed in the hold filling baskets, each of which contained 1¼ cwt. Another four were on deck standing at the foot

---

[1] A report from the *Morning Chronicle* reprinted in the *Newcastle Journal*, 5 January 1850.

[2] H.Y. Moffat, *From Ship's-Boy to Skipper* (Paisley, 1910).

of what was called a "way" - a sort of wide ladder some four to five feet high. A derrick was arranged above the hold with a gin block at its head through which was rove a rope runner to which the baskets of coal were hooked. The hauling end of the runner divided into four ends at a height of about twenty feet above deck level. These ends were called "bell ropes." Each grasping a "bell rope" the four whippers would, in unison, skip up the "way" hauling in their ropes as they ascended, rather like a mountain climber hauling himself up a rock face, then when on the top rung they would jump together in perfect synchronization, their combined weight propelling the basket of coal upwards. Once clear of the hold it was grabbed by a "basket man" (usually the foreman) who was waiting on a plank laid across the hatch. Taking advantage of the momentum caused by the "jump" he would run, guiding the basket and upsetting it into a weighing machine. The machine was like a large coal scuttle connected to a scale. When a weight of 2½ cwts (two basket fulls) had been deposited a luminary called the "coal meter" discharged the contents of the weighing machine into a barge moored alongside. The coal-whippers did their work in absolute silence, nothing was heard but the rattle of the "gin block," the discharge of coal into weighing machine and from machine to barge.

The practice of "jumping" out a cargo of coal was not the sole preserve of the London coal-whippers. It was the method used by the collier crews they had to discharge their own cargoes as was frequently the case. One Tyne owned collier, with a crew of eight, "jumped" out 100 tons a day at Hamburg during the 1850's.

The Life

Work aboard a Nineteenth Century sailing ship seems to have been incredibly hard when compared with the standards of the present day. Everything was "pully-haul," without powered aids of any kind. There was the frequent need to pump ship, work cargo, weigh anchor and go aloft (120 feet to the fore-royal yard of the Amble owned *Meggie Dixon*) to handle sails. Four hours on and four hours off, with a "dog watch" in between, was the watch pattern of the day. The watch below could be called out as often as the demands of the ship required, which was frequent. Couple the hard work to cold, severe weather, little sleep, and a leaky ship it is easy to understand why the phrase: "Put in. Crew exhausted" was often met with in the *Shipping Intelligence* columns of the time.

Walter Runciman, who worked his way up from an apprentice on the Blyth brig *Harperly* to become one of the North-East's most prominent shipowner's gives some idea of how the crews were trained, how they lived and what conditions were like:

> "...during the winter months I learned every landmark, buoy and swirl of the tide on the Coast from Blyth to the Tyne to London, and the French coasting ports of Calais and Boulogne; the London

trade during contrary winds and icy nights tiding it from Yarmouth to Gravesend; dropping the anchor and heaving it up with hand spikes at the change of every tide; the handling of the ropes when tacking from side to side of the channel, caused festering gashes in the joints of our hands. In addition to this, the pumps and heaving the lead were actively kept going."[1]

When wind or tide did not serve to advantage, a sailing ship had little option but to come to anchor if she wanted to save what progress had been achieved. Before reaching the Thames the *Sally* had anchored on five occasions. On 16 June she dropped anchor in 10 fathoms. To lie in safety about thirty fathoms of chain (180 feet) would have had to be run out. To get this in again was a slow, hard, back breaking job. The only power available would have been an "Armstrong's patent" windlass. This primitive apparatus was an integral part of a wooden ship's construction and consisted of a couple of timbers projecting above the deck, in the bow of the vessel, which supported a ratcheted barrel between them. Three turns of the anchor cable were taken around this barrel which was fitted with whelps of timber or iron to give the chain a better grip. The whole contraption was worked by either handspikes being inserted in holes in the roller or a couple of levers. In addition to the heavy labour of moving these levers up and down, see-saw fashion or working the spikes, crews often received a good drenching especially when weighing anchor in an open roadstead with water shooting up the hawse pipes and icy spray whipping aboard. A well-scrubbed handspike, for use with these primitive windlasses, as one of the tools of a collier seaman's trade which he carried tied to the outside of his bag of clothes. In his *Collier Brigs & their Sailors*, Runciman catalogues the evils which were common on small sailing ships:

"...drudgery hard usage, inferior food, cramped unhealthy accommodation." He had his fair share and described one ship which: "in stormy weather shivered and shook as though she were falling to pieces. Her forecastle deck used to open and shut like bellows, and every plunge or roll she took gave the impression that she splitting in two. The oiled tent covers that were stretched from head to foot of our canvas hammocks could not prevent some of the water getting on to the pillows, and "donkey's breakfast". It availed nothing to growl about having to take what sleep we could on wet bedding, or about having to pump or sink. We had to go through with it."

---

[1] Walter Runciman, *Sunbeam II in 1930* (Newcastle upon Tyne, 1930).

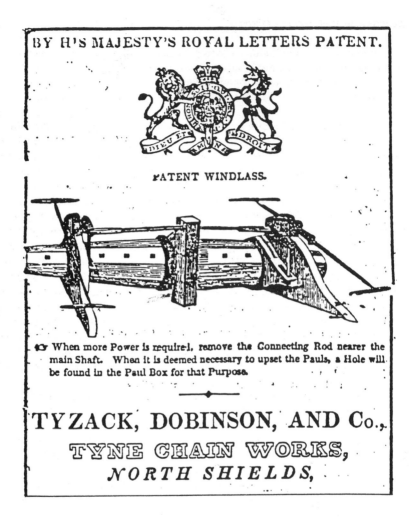

BY H'S MAJESTY'S ROYAL LETTERS PATENT.

PATENT WINDLASS.

☞ When more Power is required, remove the Connecting Rod nearer the main Shaft. When it is deemed necessary to upset the Pauls, a Hole will be found in the Paul Box for that Purpose.

TYZACK, DOBINSON, AND Co.,
TYNE CHAIN WORKS,
NORTH SHIELDS,

At the time of the publication of this advertisement in 1841, upwards of 1,200 vessels had been fitted with the Tyzack, Dobinson & Company's windlass. Similar types were to be found aboard sailing vessels trading, and being built, well into the Twentieth Century. They were operated by the levers, illustrated in the advertisement, or by handspikes inserted in the holes visible on the barrel (see also explanation of Armstrong's Patent in the Glossary).

9

Murder on the *Meggie Dixon*

When Runciman alluded to "drudgery hard usage" perhaps he had in mind the tragic events which took place aboard the Amble barque *Meggie Dixon* - events to which he was contemporaneous.

Registering 474 tons, with a length of just under 145 feet,, the *Meggie Dixon* ranked amongst the more superior Amble owned ships. She was probably considered by the seafaring community to be an "Indiaman" - a sobriquet used to describe a better class of merchantman which voyaged east of the Cape of Good Hope. She certainly earned some handsome freights for her owners in the Eastern Trades. It was one such voyage which brought her terrible notoriety.

Described as a "quiet, good natured fellow", Charles Ashley Cooper was twenty-one years of age. What made him give up his job as a chemist's assistant to embark on a seafaring career at an age which, in those days, would be considered rather old is not recorded. Perhaps the sight of the bonny barque, bound to the "Exotic East," appealed to some spirit of adventure or romanticism. If it was, he was soon to be sadly disillusioned.

The *Meggie Dixon*, under the command of Richard Proudfoot, left Sunderland on 1 May 1875 with Cooper on board. His ignorance of ships and the ways of the sea soon became apparent. Saddled with this inexperienced young man at the beginning of a long voyage, William Strickland, the mate to whose watch he was assigned, began to vent his anger in a particularly vicious manner even as the barque made her way down the Wear. He was aided by James Murray, the bosun, while Capt. Proudfoot did nothing to protect Cooper and even joined in the beatings and indignities he was later subjected to.

Subsequent court evidence described how Cooper was frequently kicked and rope's-ended, the blows being landed on the back of his neck causing him to bleed from nose and ears; he was driven to the masthead and made to make sounds like a cuckoo; his hair was cut off and the bare head covered with grease; was made to strip and lie in the scuppers where water was dashed over him and a scrubbing given with a new broom; to march, when nearly when nearly naked, like a soldier with a capstan bar instead of a rifle; made to shovel coal in the dark, enclosed fore-peak for over twenty-four hours without food and water. Whenever the mate or bosun met him on deck, Cooper became the recipient of a beating.

The catalogue of ill treatment went on. Suffering from scurvy, starved until he: "looked like a skeleton", escape from his tormentors and their floating hell came on the morning of 4 August when the wind freshened. Orders were given to reef top-sails. As he went to climb aloft Cooper was hurried along by the bosun with blows to his neck and ribs. By this time: "he looked ill and like a skeleton." Once in the rigging he was heard to cry: "Oh, God! leave me alone; oh, Lord, do!" Soon after came the shout "Man overboard" - it was Cooper. The cook saw him in the water; his face was bleeding. A sea rolled over him; he was seen no more.

"Man overboard!"

Instead of immediately throwing a life-bouy to him, the captain and bosun wasted time fastening a line to it. Twenty vital minutes were to elapse before it went overboard. More attention seems to have been given to preserving the buoy than saving the man! Although the *Meggie Dixon* was brought up to the wind, no attempt to lower a boat was made. By that time she must have been anything up to a couple of miles from the drowning apprentice.

It was not until the barque put into Falmouth, at the end of her voyage to the East Indies, that Capt. Proudfoot, his mate and bosun were arrested and charged with manslaughter.

The case caused intense excitement in the Cornish port. A crowd of two thousand turned up for the hearing. A near riot developed, with threats of lynching being shouted at the prisoners. Remanded in custody, they were eventually tried before the Bodmin Assizes in the following July. Found not guilty of manslaughter, but convicted for wounding, Capt. Proudfoot was imprisoned for one year, the mate and bosun got five years apiece.

At the trial it was revealed that Strickland, the mate, had shouted on one occasion: "Move along, you have no business to go to sea to take the bread out of a poor mans' mouth". This outburst, impregnated as it was with connotations of class resentment, no doubt alluded to Cooper's background. Although both his parents were dead, he appeared to have had a comfortable upbringing. His brother, who was described as Cooper's "guardian", was a man of some substance, a director of the London Trading Bank no less. It was he who brought the charges against Capt. Proudfoot and his officers. Whether charges would have been brought at all if Cooper had come from a less well placed family is open to conjecture.

The only member of the crew to protest against the Cooper's treatment was Fritze Rotcke, the cook/steward. He approached Capt. Proudfoot on two occasions and prophetically remarked that: "he (the captain) might ruin himself for life if he did not do something." Proudfoot did order his officers to stop the beatings and even went so far as to threaten the mate that he would: "knock him off duty" if he persisted. However a sinister rider was added: "they (the officers) might do as they liked to the rest of the crew!" Cooper's reprieve was short-lived.

When Proudfoot found that Cooper had developed scurvy his initial reaction was to give him yet another rope's-ending, to teach him: "what scurvy was". Fritze Rotcke was ordered to give a: "double allowance of lime juice", to rub his sores with a mixture of: "vinegar and lime juice" and "no food but rice and barley". Ominously the crew were told that if they gave Cooper any food: "he (the captain) would starve them to". On another occasion, when Rotcke remonstrated with the mate, he threatened to: "choke him and stop his jaw"[1].

Intimidated by these threats, the crew just kept their heads down and got on with their jobs, while their hapless shipmate suffered. It is easy to sit in our comfortable homes and call them spineless.

Shipwreck and Disaster

Forty-seven per cent of the vessels listed in this work are known to have been lost by marine peril while Aln or Coquet owned. Large though this percentage seems, it was modest by the standards of the time. A recent publication quotes seventy-five percent as about the average![2] Here are some statistics of losses around the British Isles, occurring in the 1850's when sail was pre-imminent:

1850	681 ships	780 lives	1851	701 ships	750 lives
1852	1100 ships	900 lives	1854	987 ships	1549 lives
1855	1141 ships	(576 on East Coast)			

The figures for 1856 are given in considerable detail:

Ship losses: East Coast 506. South Coast 119. Scilly Isles 12. West Coast 307. Isle of Man 5. Lundy 11. Northern Isles 38.

Total: 1153 (229,936 tons).

Causes: Stress of weather 148. Unseaworthy 37. Mistaking lights 10. Fog or current 38. Defective charts 3. Errors of judgement 12. Errors of pilot: 7. Want of pilot 3. Want of caution 11. Interference 2. Defective compasses 5. Ignorance of coast 3. Neglect of the lead 21. General negligence 9.

Amongst those lost were 139 colliers and 34 steam ships; 484 were insured.

---

[1] Quotations from the *Meggie Dixon* trial are as reported in the *Newcastle Daily Journal* various issues, particularly those of 23 & 25 April 1878.

[2] *Nourse Line* by F.W. Perry & W.A. Laxton (Kendal, 1991)

The high proportion wrecked on the East Coast does not necessarily imply that the area was more dangerous than anywhere else. What it does reflect is the number of passages being made between the northern coal ports and London in particular. Only one violent storm from the east could add dramatically to the figures. On 7 January 1854 a severe east-south-east gale blew up catching a large number of colliers which had left London the previous day and others which were making their way northwards after being windbound in the Yarmouth Roads. When the storm subsided it was found that 200 sailing vessels had been driven ashore between Lowestoft and the Leith Roads - 43 between the Wear and Aln, including nine off the mouths of the Aln and Coquet. Amongst these was the fifty-two year old schooner *Telemachus* belonging to Edward Whitfield and various members of the Turnbull family of Amble. She was later re-floated, but the coal laden North Shields brig *Earl of Newburgh,* which had been driven from an anchorage in the Coquet Roads, became a total loss. She had previously belonged to Thomas Browne, one of the leading lights in the creation of Warkworth Harbour.

Of the other seven vessels, three became total losses: the brig *Monarch* of Guernsey, which stranded near the *Earl of Newburgh*; the Danish galliot *Catherine Maria*, wrecked in Duridge Bay, and an unidentified Spanish vessel which drove ashore on Boulmer Rocks with no one on board. The remainder were got off.

It is an ill wind which blows no good. That single gale had taken 100 vessels out of the east-coast coal trade. The freight rates to London went up to 15/-(75p); terms for re-floating vessels rose from £40 to £120 and shipwrights were asking for an extra 1/-(5p) a day to repair damage!

The worst tragedy (other than those which went "missing") to befall an Amble ship happened to the inaptly named *Grace Darling.* A Prince Edward Island built barque she had traded world-wide before becoming Amble owned at the end of her career. After being driven helplessly before a howling gale, up the East Coast of Scotland, she went ashore just north of Rattary Head with the loss of fourteen of her crew. The tragedy was compounded by the loss of four men who were washed out of the Stonehaven life-boat which had been launched in an attempt to render assistance. An inquiry into the wrecking of the *Grace Darling* came up with the controversial opinion that her loss was caused by mismanagement and the crew being given liberal issues of grog.

In the four years leading up to 1850, eighty-seven British ships were: "burnt by accident", eleven by coal cargoes igniting, seven were "blown up by coal dust", one by spontaneous combustion, and four by "gas." Surprising, considering that coal was the cargo most carried by the Aln/Coquet vessels, only one of them (the brigantine *Wave Spirit*) is known to have been lost by burning. It happened off Seaham Harbour.

Perhaps the most melancholy way for a ship to end her life was to be posted "missing" - simply to leave port and disappear off the face of the earth. Of this catastrophe Joseph Conrad wrote in his *Mirror of the Sea:*

"Nothing of her ever comes to light - no grating, no lifebuoy, no piece of boat or branded oar - to give a hint of the place and date of her of her sudden end"..."How did she do it? In the word "missing" there is a horrible depth of doubt and speculation. Did she go quickly from under the men's feet, or did she resist to the end, letting the sea batter her to pieces, start her butts, wrenching her frame, load her with an increasing weight of salt water, and, dismasted, unmanageable, rolling heavily, her boats gone, her decks swept, had she wearied her men half to death with the unceasing labour at the pumps before she sank with them like a stone."

The crew of the Alnmouth snow *Sun* watched helplessly as a deep laden sloop went to "the port of missing ships" twelve miles off the Tyne on a wild day in 1864. Earlier this vessel had been sighted lying about half-a-mile off the *Sun's* weather beam. A tremendous lurch made the snow's crew hang on for dear life. She recovered from the welter of wind, sea and spray just in time for them to see the masthead of the sloop disappearing beneath the sea. The severity of the weather made it impossible to beat to windward to search for survivors. Nobody knew her name or nationality; where she was bound to or from. Someone, somewhere, would have been waiting for a father, son, husband or sweetheart who would never come home from the sea.

At least five Aln/Coquet sailing ships are known to have suffered this sad fate. The largest of them was the *Aydon Forest,* a fine 500 ton Alnwick owned barque She disappeared after leaving Mobile, Alabama, on 20 July 1889. The others were the *Jane & Eleanor, Rambler, Sir William Wallace* and *Nymphen.*

What does not seem to appear in the published statistics of the era is the number of men and boys who were injured, killed or washed overboard. Some ships had the sinister reputation of killing a man every voyage. One of the best known of the Amble built and owned ships, the snow *Gloriana,* had three crew members washed overboard in the course of a disastrous maiden voyage.

In the mainly *laissez-faire* commercial conditions of the Nineteenth Century, there was little in the way of compensation for injured seamen or the families of those lost. Christie Schofield writing in the *Sea Breezes* magazine of May 1947 described how, fifty-eight years before, he had left the Tyne on the coal laden barque *Arethusa*[1] (Capt. Hamilton) bound for the West Coast of South America as a keen, able bodied first trip apprentice and returned a few months later: "disillusioned, aged beyond his years by intense physical and mental hardship, and having suffered the loss of both his feet."

The *Arethusa* had been abandoned on fire near the Falkland Islands. Ten days were spent in an open boat, in sub-Antarctic temperatures, before being picked up by the Glasgow barque *Lady Octavia*. In the meantime young Scho-

---

[1] The *Arethusa* was an iron barque of 1,339 gross tons, built at Greenock in 1869 by R. Steele & Co. She was owned by Capt. Hamilton and his brother.

field's feet had become frost bitten and gangrenous (they were later amputated at Valparaiso), the negro cook had died, the mate lost his reason, and another apprentice lay unconscious. He and the mate died aboard the rescue ship which took a further thirty-nine days to get them to Valparaiso. The captain and steward of the *Arethusa* had died aboard a second boat which made Port Stanley, in the Falkland Islands.

Schofield's account finishes with the following paragraph: "Arrived ashore. I enquired as to the shipowner, the surviving partner (the *Arethusa's* late master was the other). My father informed me that the office was closed down, and there was no trace of the firm's representative. I may say that he had disclaimed all responsibility for me after I had left the ships side."

And so it was. Once a seaman had left his ship, whatever the circumstances, his wages ceased and apparently any responsibility for his well being. The exception was when a ship was sold. Even so it needed a court order to get Hugh Andrews, to pay the wages of his crew for the time it took them to get home after he had sold his *Camperdown* (Amble's biggest sailing ship) at Sydney, Cape Breton. She had put in there after being damaged in a collision. Andrews contention was that she had been "wrecked" which, if substantiated, would have saved him considerable expense.

If the work was so hard and dangerous why did anyone go to sea? The only answer can be that working conditions ashore at the time were probably no better or worse than those aboard ship. Indeed there was the case of a young woman who left her employment in a rope factory, disguised herself as a boy, and went to sea aboard a Sunderland collier because she found that her male seafaring contemporaries were better paid and better fed than she was! For a working class North-East boy the alternatives were either coal mining, the heavy industry of Tyneside, or agriculture. Capt. Charles Henry Deacon, who commanded the Fowey owned barquentine *Waterwitch* (the last cargo carrying square-rigger to be registered in a United Kingdom port) for many years, had a stock answer for anyone who grumbled about the hard work: "You don't know what hard work is until you've been on a farm." He knew what he was talking about. Deacon had spent his early working life as a farmers boy!

Alnmouth

> The name Alemouth is used in a number of the older shipping registers and publications. Just how this came about is explained with tongue-in-cheek succinctness in the *History of Northumberland Directory for 1887*: "This name may be termed corruption refined. By provincial usage Alnmouth became Yalmouth. But Yal is Ale; hence Yalmouth is Alemouth; and such has been the English name!"

The rivers Aln and Coquet empty into the North Sea, some three miles apart, from the ruggedly beautiful coastline of Northumberland. Not far from their mouths lie the historic towns of Alnwick, on the Aln, and Warkworth, on the Coquet. Both were of immense importance in the medieval history of the British Isles. Beneath the ramparts of their embattled castles the fates of kings and ancient nations were decided. The turbulent times past. The swords were beaten into ploughshares. Alnwick became the regional centre for the corn trade.

Five miles downstream from Alnwick lies the resort village of Alnmouth. On a recent train journey from Berwick to Newcastle, the track of which passes nearby, the author over-heard a lady passenger describe Alnmouth as a "jewel." A more apt description would be difficult to find. Perched on a headland, on the north side of Aln Harbour, its unspoilt profile still possesses many of the characteristics which would have been familiar to seaman of the Victorian era as they cautiously crossed the bar of the Aln aboard their diminutive sloops, brigs, snows and schooners.

Alnmouth's recorded history, as a port, goes back as far as the Thirteenth Century. In 1296 its harbour was described as providing: "good anchorage to vessels engaged in foreign trade." Its importance as a port became apparent in times of war. In 1316 the bailiff of Alemouth was ordered was ordered to send ships sufficiently: "munitioned and victualled to go to Gascony." Ten years later all of the port's ships able to carry 30 tons of cargo or more, were commanded to be: "at Orewell, in Suffolk, sufficiently armed and victualled for the defense of the Kingdom."[1] Similar edicts were made in 1333, 1334 and 1336.

The rural harbour had prospects of becoming a coal port in 1533 when George Clarkson, an Alnwick trader, took the lease of a mine at Bilton. The terms of the lease stipulated that coal should be loaded at "Alynemouth" for "carrying away...to his most advantage." However the scheme does not appear to have materialised and it was corn, not coal, that was to make Alnmouth's name some centuries later.

When John Wesley, the theologian, evangelist and founder of Methodism called during 1748 he wrote in his journal: "We rode to Alemouth, a small

---

[1] George Tate, 'An Account of Lesbury Parish, Northumberland', *History of the Berwick-shire Naturalists Club*, Vol 8, (1879).

Alnmouth at the end of the Nineteenth Century. The sailing ships have gone. The vessel in the foreground is the 63 ton barge *Arrow*, owned by the Tyne Wherry Company of Newcastle. She would probably have been towed around from the Tyne, or Blyth, with a cargo of coal.

(From an old postcard)

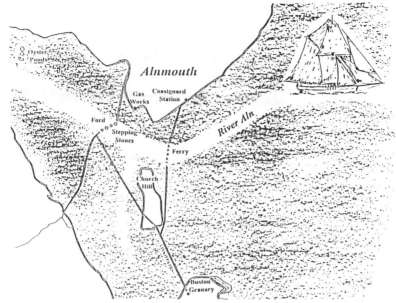

Alnmouth Harbour in about 1860.

seaport and town famous for all kinds of wickedness". What he was visiting was a sailors town which no doubt possessed all the entertainments and temptations which enliven such places. Small and wicked it may have been but prosperous it certainly was. Prosperous enough to attracted the attention of predators in the shape of privateers. In the year before Wesley's visit a smack had been captured off the harbour entrance and then ransomed for £250. Aboard was a young surgeon making his way to London in the hope of getting a berth on an East Indiaman. He was relieved of £20 in cash and clothes which he valued at a further £30 - substantial amounts in those days. He came ashore: "in a melancholy condition, and had not so much as a coat left, save a wide one, that he wore above his night gown and had a wig left him, and in that condition rode home to Berwick next day".[2]

A great fillip to the importance of Alnmouth came in the mid-1750's with the completion of a turnpike road from the corn producing farm lands of Hexhamshire. Large granaries were erected to store the staple while it awaited shipment. The ships, which came to collect it, brought roof slates from Holland, timber and guano - a much sought after fertilizer. All this had to be stored and distributed. The Hexham, or Corn Road as it is sometimes referred to, must have been a busy thoroughfare.

During the Christmas of 1806, a great storm struck the area. Masses of water surged down the Aln washing away bridges and causeways and cutting off some of the vital granaries, guano sheds and sawmill from the rest of the town before busting through the sand dunes into the sea. The Aln had changed

---

[2]   Edward Bateson, B.A., *A History of Northumberland*, Vol 2, (Newcastle, 1895).

An unidetified brigantine lying in Alnmouth Harbour. Under sail she would have set a deep, single topsail and bentinick-foresail to help when beating about in busy, narrow waterways such as the Thames.

its course. The harbour silted up, the bar at the entrance changed so much with every natural disturbance that no lead marks could be given.

Despite these difficulties, small merchant sailing ships still made their way in, right up until the latter years of the Nineteenth Century. A shipping list of 1841 notes that the 63 ton schooner *Croft* (Capt. George Potter) was employed as a regular trader to Newcastle. The schooner *Express* voyaged to London. Sometimes she called at Amble on the southward passage for a cargo of coal but usually return with "goods." She was still doing this into the 1850's by which time the little port had been reached by the ever mushrooming railway system. The *Croft* and *Express* (Capt. Gibb) were locally owned. For five years following her acquisition by William Robertson, a timber merchant who lived in Narrowgate Street, Alnwick, the old brigantine *Peace* regularly brought cargoes of wood direct to Alnmouth from Gothenburg. From 1830 onwards some fifty-three ships belonged to people living in or near the port. Over 40% of these were schooners and sloops measuring less than 100 tons. The largest was the 586 ton barque *Manfred*, belonged to Alnwick owners.

Navigating in and out of the little harbour was fraught with difficulty. On 24 August 1835 the snow *Good Agreement* (belonging to a South Shields publican), inward bound from Littlehampton, got ashore at the entrance. A contemporary newspaper report noted: "if weather proves fine she may be got off next tide." She was got off, only to be wrecked a couple of years later with the loss of two of her crew. Four months after this incident the 99 ton brig *Marquess of Wellington,* belonging to Edward Gibb of Alnmouth, struck the shifting bar when outward bound and: "continued beating all that tide" ending up smashing her keel and doing other bottom damage. Some cargo had to be discharged to get her afloat and back into the safety of the harbour. Serious though these incidents were, they were probably no worse than what happened at the mouth of any port in those days. In 1841 the rates of insurance from the Tyne to Blyth, Seaton Sluice, Amble and Alnmouth were exactly the same - 7/6d (37·5p) per cent.

However the little port's final death knell seems to have been rung in 1896 when a visiting brig (the *Joanna)* sustained damage to her hull after rolling over into the channel while discharging a cargo of timber - "After this no one would insure a freight into Alnmouth."[1]

---

[1] Robert Simper, *North East Sail* (Newton Abbot, 1975).

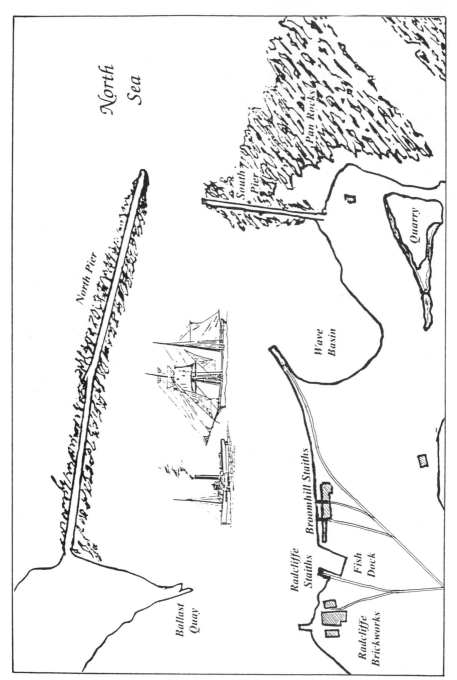

Warkworth Harbour at the end of the sailing ship era.
(Map by R.E. Keys)

North Sea

North Pier

Ballast Quay

Radcliffe Staiths

Radcliffe Brickworks

Fish Dock

Broomhill Staiths

Wave Basin

Quarry

South Pier

Pan Rocks

Amble (Warkworth Harbour)

> The name Warkworth Harbour is that given in the 1837 Act of Parliament authorising the construction of a harbour at the entrance to the Coquet. However all loading and discharging, the business of the port, and customs transactions took place at Amble.

The 1831 Census gave Amble a population of 247. Sixty years later, when the last of the locally owned sailing ships were being disposed of, it had increased more than tenfold. The cause of this rise was the construction of a harbour, built specifically for the shipment of coal, at the entrance to the River Coquet.

Coal is known to have been produced in the area from as early as 1566 when the tenants of two collieries paid 8s.2d. (41p) and 12s. (60p) per annum respectively for the privilege of extracting it. Just when the first cargo of the fuel was loaded on the Coquet is difficult to determine. In 1832 when Hamilton Fulton, an engineer, put forward proposals for the construction of a harbour at the river's entrance, he refers to Gibbon's Staith which suggests that coal, taken from workings at Togston, was being loaded then, and possibly had been for some period before. At that time the waters of the Coquet were: "being allowed to find their way to the sea as best they could through the sands of the shore."[1]

As can be imagined it was a dangerous procedure for a sailing ship to make its way into the mouth of such a river. An exposed entrance, shifting bar, and tortuous, shallow channel, would not have endeared the Coquet to either ship masters, ship owners or underwriters. Only very small vessels could hope to run the gauntlet of such navigational hazards with any chance of success. Commercial considerations called for much better facilities.

In about 1835 Robert Kingscote & Thomas Browne (soon to become a substantial shipowner) obtained a lease from the Earl of Newburgh to mine for coal at Hauxley, about two kilometres south-east of Amble. A colliery was opened and given the name Radcliffe (the family name of the Earl of Newburgh). A railway was constructed to the Coquet, at Amble, where a staith was built to load the coal into ships.

As coal production from the Radcliffe Colliery increased, safe access to the sea became imperative. In 1837 an Act of Parliament was passed to enable a harbour to be built at Pan Haven at the entrance to the Coquet. Commissioners were appointed to administer the project - the Warkworth Harbour Commission. They were the Earl of Newburgh (there was a schooner named after him) and the Trustees of his estate, two lessees of the Radcliffe Colliery, three nominees of the Duke of Northumberland and ten other gentlemen. Civil engineers were invited to submit plans and, on the advice of Sir John Rennie (son of the famous

---

[1] Thomas Meik & Sons, *A Historical Account of Warkworth Harbour* (Edinburgh, 1883).

Warkworth Harbour looking seaward. A brigantine lies in the foreground, and a diverse collection of sailing craft are moored in the stream. Photograph probably taken in the 1890's.

(Author's collection)

Scottish civil engineer), an amalgam of similar proposals put forward by John Murray of Sunderland and James Leslie were accepted.

Basically they called for the construction of two stone piers. On the north side of the entrance was to be one extending in an easterly direction for some 2,000 feet to give protection from fury of the frequent north-easterly winds and seas. The second pier was to strike northwards from Pan Point for 600 feet, leaving a space of 250 feet between their ends through which vessels would pass into a straightened channel leading to a line of quays on the south side of the river at Amble. Kingscote and Browne, the Radcliffe Colliery lessees, were awarded the £46,000 for its construction. The 1837 Act had stipulated that the project was to be completed in five years but a subsequent Act, passed in 1842, increased this for a further five.

A lot of money had to be spent on re-building the north pier. Originally constructed of sandstone, quarried locally, it was no match for the battering the North Sea had to offer. Eventually whinstone, carried from Scotland by sea, had to be substituted. Shipping Intelligence reports of the early 1850's indicate that the *Diligence* (Capt. Deas), *Aid* (Capt. Brown) and *Propitious* (Capt. Baker) all arrived at Amble with stones from Leith.

In time staiths serving the Radcliffe and Broomhill collieries were constructed along with a fish dock and cargo berths used mainly for the loading of bricks manufactured at the Radcliffe Brickworks. The expense of this building and re-building, plus the burden of maintenance, burnt holes in the pockets of the original bond holders. When completed in 1854 the harbour had cost them a hefty £184,800 and despite a marked increase in coal shipments (33,000 tons in 1845 to 80,000 tons in 1860) the return on their capital outlay was minuscule. They off-loaded their interest for what was said to be a mere £8,000 to the owners of the Radcliffe Colliery which, since the year the harbour had been completed, had belonged to Joseph & John Harrison and Carl Lange. As well as being mine and harbour owners, this trio were also joint owners of the brig *Derwentwater* in addition to other vessels.

During this period, progress with the development of Amble as a harbour had stagnated. Much of the collieries output was taken by rail to Tyne Dock and South Dock, Sunderland, for tran-shipment. It was still limited to taking ships of no more than about 300 tons. New virility came from across the Irish Sea with the arrival of Hugh Andrews, from Belfast, as owner of the Broomhill Colliery (it had began production in about 1840). He was soon to spot the potential of the little port as a desirable addition to his coal field acquisitions. In 1869 he acquired a major stake in the harbour company and was soon to become sole owner. Under his direction important improvements were implemented. The South Pier was almost re-built. A dredger was bought, the depth of water on the bar and at the loading berths was increased - in 1885 it was 10 to 12 feet for vessels lying alongside; ten years later vessels drawing 20 feet could load under the coal spouts. With these improvements trade increased. Ships of 1,400 to 1,500 tons could, by then, safely visit the port.

In the decade leading up to the sale of the *Gloriana* in 1896, the last locally owned windjammer of the Victorian Era, Amble was visited by 2,238 sailing ships and 5,058 steamers which, together, carried away 3,207,158 tons of coal. Also shipped were bricks, fire-clay and herrings; the main imports were pit-props, deals and other timber.

Amble's life as a coal port came to an end on 25 September 1969 when the motor vessels *Ferryhill* and *Jonrix* took aboard the last shipments. The staiths at which they loaded were soon afterwards dismantled. Nowadays, it is mainly fishing vessels and yachts which enter the Coquet.

The 98 ton ketch rigged barge *Europa* of Rochester and a topsail schooner lie alongside dolphins in Warkworth Harbour in the mid-1890's. The *Europa* was built at Sittingbourne, Kent, in 1871 and had originally been rigged as a schooner.These big barges were destined to become the last of sailing colliers.
(From an old postcard)

Warkworth Harbour viewed from the east. The brigantine in the foreground is the 146 ton *Amilhujo* of Wyk-auf-Fohr, in the Frisian Islands. Beginning in 1878, she carried a number of coal cargoes from Amble to her home port. Other Wyk vessels employed in this trade were the schooners *Henriette* and *Die Gute Euvestay*.
(Courtesy: Newcastle City Libraries)

Another view of the *Amilhujo*, lying capsized on a sandbank near the island of Oland in 1895. She was built in 1872 at Sandefjord, Norway, and belonged to to L. Heymann & Söbne of Wyk.
(From an old postcard)

Coquet Ship Builders

In his book *Amble and District,* T.L. McAndrews states that: "The first ship to have been built at Amble dates back to the eighteenth Century. About this time enormous quantities of oak trees were cut down in Chevington Wood.. and with this timber a vessel was constructed on the Coquet Banks near the old "granary" on the Warkworth road, and was named the *Chevington Oak.*"

The only vessel I have come across with a name anything like this is the 145 ton brig *Chivington Oak* which, according to her Newcastle Custom House Register, was not Coquet but Aln built. The register gives her year of build as 1811. Blyth owned from 1814 she was wrecked near Dunkirk on 31 August 1833.

Whatever the truth of the matter, after the establishment of Amble as a port, fourteen sailing ships are known to have been constructed on the banks of the Coquet between 1839 and 1862. The first of these was built by George Surtees who came from Monkwearmouth, near Sunderland. The most prominent ship-builders were James Sanderson and Thomas Leighton who constructed seven ships the largest of which was the 257 ton clipper-barque *Sunrise,* built for London owners. Here is a list of the vessels and their builders:

George Surtees

1839	*Breeze*	schooner	136 tons
1839	*Trader*	sloop	48 tons
1840	*Duchess of Northumberland*	schooner	65 tons
1841	*Aid*	brig	189 tons

John Bergen

1851	*Landscape*	brig	185 tons

Thomas Leighton

1852	*Perseverance*	barque	293 tons

James Sanderson (died 21 June 1859) & Thomas Leighton

1855	*Providence*	brig	194 tons
1856	*Isabella & Mary*	brig	202 tons
1859	*Amble*	snow	142 tons
1859	*Sunrise*	barque	257 tons
1860	*Gloriana*	snow	169 tons
1861	*Agenoria*	snow	176 tons

Builder Unknown

1863	*Luck's All*	schooner	26 tons

D.A. Douglas

1867	*Tulip*	schooner	101 tons

(Further details of these vessels are given in the *Fleet List*)

With the completion of the *Tulip*, shipbuilding ceased on the Coquet until the demand for tonnage created by the First World War brought it back for a brief spell. The Amble Ferro-Concrete Company was registered early in 1918 with a capital of £25,000. The principles behind its formation were G.M. Ritchie and A.N. Gowan, respectively Chairman and Managing Director of the well known Palmer's Shipbuilding & Iron Company of Jarrow-on-Tyne. The objectives of the firm were to become ship builders, repairers and owners. They began by building a couple of 306 gross ton concrete tugs - the *Cretebow* and *Cretestem* for the Shipping Controller. The *Cretebow* was launched on 31 July 1919. In the Palmer's Company report, published in September 1920, it was noted that: "the shipyard at Amble...is being adapted for building steel vessels of a smaller type than those built at Jarrow and Hebburn." Amongst the steel vessels constructed were the tug *Anglo-Mex 101*, and two passenger/vehicle ferries for Jarrow Corporation, the *Jarrow* and *A.B. Gowan*. The author well remembers the *A.B. Gowan* as she made her way, back and forwards, across the Tyne between Jarrow and Howdon with ponderous reliability. This splendid old ship's career ended during October 1967 when she was delivered to the ship-breaking yard of Clayton & Davie, at Dunston-on-Tyne, after forty-six years of service.

While shipbuilding came and went on the Coquet, boat building has remained a constant industry since the Harrison Brothers established a yard in 1870. Trading for over a century, they gained a splendid reputation building the traditional fishing cobles as well as a variety of other small craft. Boat building at Amble is nowadays carried out by the firm of Marshall Branson who recently built a very sophisticated, 18 tonne, aluminium, cable laying barge for use in Icelandic waters.

Epilogue to Sail

For the most part, merchant sailing ships were an unpredictable and often uncomfortable mode of transport. When an economically viable, more reliable, alternative presented itself passengers and shippers were quick to desert them.

By the 1830's steamships, with their tall smoke belching funnels and thrashing paddles, had become part of the maritime scene on the North-East Coast. In 1830 you could have boarded the steamship *Ardincaple* at Newcastle Quay for a passage to Leith, or the *Tourist* for a run to London. In the July of 1835 a weekend break was available aboard the *Nicholas* from Newcastle Quay to Warkworth and Alnmouth - 2/6d (25p) for the return journey. Newspaper advertisements indicated fairly precise departure times.

Where a steamer was available, passengers were no longer totally dependant on the vagaries of the wind to reach their destinations. Sea journeys became reasonably predictable. No longer was there any need to waste days, weeks or even months "knocking about" in the North Sea. As late as 1894 a South Shields brigantine took 44 days to sail from Littlehampton, on the South Coast, to her home port!

While the steamers made great inroads into the coastal passenger trades the voracious coal consuming appetites of their primitive engines left little room for cargo carrying. So far as the coal trade from the North-East was concerned the sailing ship was to remain supreme until the advent of the purpose built steam collier *John Bowes,* an iron hulled screw driven vessel, constructed by Palmer, Brothers & Company at Jarrow, in 1852. Within a year of her commissioning, regional newspapers were carrying reports of a coal trade drawing away from its traditional reliance on sail driven tonnage. The *Newcastle Journal* quoted: "One screw steamer, such as now engaged in the traffic, will in one year carry a greater quantity of coals to London than ten collier ships of the average burthen can do in the same period." There was a momentary reprieve for the sailing collier during the Crimean War, when the Government chartered many of the steamers, but the die had been well and truly cast. By the 1870's only about a quarter on London's coal was being delivered in the holds of sailing ships.

In many ways, certainly so far as the coastal sailing ship was concerned, the growth of the railway system had as much to do with their decline than the steam ship. A glance at a railway map for 1852 shows an interlinking system covering much of the United Kingdom. Only the north of Scotland, West Wales and the north coasts of Devon and Cornwall seemed to have escaped this transport revolution. The North-East coast was well catered for with a coast hugging route from Newcastle to Edinburgh. Direct rail communication between London and Newcastle had been established by 1844. Three years later it was extended to Berwick, passing close to Amble and Alnmouth. In January 1850: "valuable TIMBER, &c. belonging to the Hull of the Prussian brig *St.Johannass,*" which had stranded on Warkworth Sands, was advertised in the *Newcastle Journal* to be sold by auction for "Ready Money." It was also noted that the timber: "is lying convenient for Removal, being...a short Distance from Warkworth Station upon the Berwick and Newcastle Railway."[1] A few years before the only way of transporting that timber would have been by coastal sailing ship or horse and cart. Gradually, over the next couple of decades and in the years that followed, branch and local lines reached many of the coastal towns which had been largely dependent on the sea for their supply of fuel and export of local produce.

Paradoxically the advent of the ocean going steamship created much employment for local sailing ships. The early steamships required frequent re-fuelling. To facilitate this, coal depots were established throughout the world and much of that coal came from the North-East in the holds of North-East sailing ships. The Amble snow *Ceylon* was bound to Port Said with coal, almost certainly destined to fill the bunkers of steamers using the newly opened Suez Canal, when she was run down and sunk off the Norfolk Coast in 1870.

Despite the competition of increasingly efficient steamships and the rapid spread of the railway system the sailing ship was a long time a dying. The last to be owned on the Coquet was the Amble built snow *Gloriana* which was sold in 1896. The Aln's long sail owning tradition had come to an end eight years before with the condemnation of the world roaming barque *Campsie Glen* at Rio de Janeiro. There was an unexpected revival in 1937 when Fountains Northumberland Trust based their topsail schooner *Penola* at Amble to help alleviate the then current unemployment problem. However she differed from her predecessors in one very significant way by having an auxiliary engine - a 50 h.p. Junkers diesel driving twin screws.

In general the sailing ship completed effectively with the steamer in the bulk carrying, long distant deep-water trades until the advent of the fuel-efficient triple expansion engine in the 1880's. But that was not the end of them by any means. By a complex variety of economic, legislative, social and geographical factors, the engine-less merchant sailing ship lingered on well into the Twentieth Century (and probably still does in the waters of some undeveloped nations). As late as 1949 the Finnish four-masted barques *Pamir* and *Passat* loaded grain in Australia's Spencer Gulf for Europe. The distinction of being the last cargo carrying, engine-less, sailing ship to trade about the British Isles, and indeed in Western Europe, goes to the 109 gross ton mulie-rigged barge *Cambria* (more popularly described as a Thames barge) which was carrying cargoes up until 1970. In her time she had hauled coal from the Humber to Harwich. The *Passat* and *Cambria* are now preserved. The *Pamir* foundered in tragic circumstances with the loss of 80 lives - mainly young lives - *after* she had had an auxiliary engine installed.

---

[1] *Newcastle Journal,* 5 January 1850.

Fleet List

For the most part, vessels included in the following list were either built in, or more than half their shares belonged to people resident in, the present (1993) administrative area of Alnwick District Council. Much information has been culled from their Custom House Registers deposited with the Northumberland, and Tyne & Wear Archives. Also included are vessels noted as being owned in the area by other sources, particularly *Lloyd's Register of Shipping* and *Amble and District* by T.L. McAndrews.

The list does not pretend to be exhaustive, nor are the ship histories as comprehensive as the author would wish. Information about any unlisted vessel, or further notes or corrections concerning the careers of individual ships, would be appreciated.

Explanation of Fleet List

Abbreviations

h.p.	Horse power	L/R	Lloyd's Register	m.f.	Manufacturer
m.m.	Master mariner	m.o.	Managing owner	O/N	Official Number
P/R	Previous registration	s.b.	Shipbuilder	s.br	Shipbroker
s.o.	Shipowner	s.w.	Shipwright		

Example
(fictitious ship)

(a) 001 *NORTHUMBRIAN PACKET* (1854-1864)   O/N 00231
(b) Barque   451 tons   125·3 x 25 x 17·7 feet
(c) *1852:* Built Sunderland by George Ratchev.
(d) *P/R:* Southampton (1852/5)
(e) **Owners** . *5.7.1854:* John Patton (32/64, s.o.), Amble; William Gallon (16/64, m.m.), Alnmouth; Cynthia McArthur (16/64, spinster), High Buston. *12.9.1860:* Thomas Watson (s.o.), Warkworth.
(f) **Masters.** *5.7.1854:* William Gallon. *12.9.1860:* Mathew Jones.
(g) A North Atlantic trader. The *Northumbrian Packet* went missing after leaving Saint John, New Brunswick, on 18 March 1864 with a cargo of timber for London

Line (a): Gives the vessel's index number relevant to this listing. Next comes the vessel's name, followed by the years (in brackets) when she was Aln/Coquet owned. Finally, at the end of the line, is the Official Number which is that given in her Custom House Register.

Line (b): Gives the ship's rig; next tonnage (registered unless otherwise stated); then dimensions: length x breadth x depth of hold. Unless otherwise stated, these details are those given in the Custom House Register at the time of build or acquisition. Tonnage is rounded up or down to the nearest ton; dimensions are expressed in feet with inches converted to decimal parts of a foot. It should be remembered that the rig, tonnage and dimensions of many ships were altered in the course of their careers, furthermore, the method of measuring ships was altered in 1836 and 1854.

Line (c): Gives date and place of build also, if known, the builders name.

Line (d): Gives the port where previously registered, if relevant, and (in brackets) the date and number of the registration.

Line (e): And the three lines following, list the owners, and (in brackets) the amount of 64th shares held, their trade, profession or social status. The dates given are those appearing on the bill of sale or, particularly in the case of newly built vessels, when first registered. When only one person is named, that person is the sole owner.

Line (f): Lists the masters and the date on which they were registered as master in the Custom House Register.

Line (g): And those following, give details of the ship's career and fate, if known.

1   **AARON EATON** (1863-1865)   O/N 3961
Brig   223 tons ֽ   106·1 x 25 x 11·9 ft.
1845: Built Saint John, New Brunswick.
P/R: Saint John, New Brunswick (1855/29).
Owners: *1845:* Aaron Eaton, Saint John, N.B. *22.4.1858:* James Smith (42/64, m.m.), Liverpool; James Sanderson & Thomas Leighton (11/64 each), both Amble shipbuilders. *21.6.1859:* James Sanderson died; his shares transferred to Isabella Sanderson (spinster), Amble. *23.4.1860:* William Smith (m.m.), Amble, acquired 16/64ths from James Smith. *23.1.1863:* James Smith (s.o.), Sunderland, acquired Isabella Sanderson's & Thomas Leighton's 11/64ths. *11.6.1863:* William Malcamson (48/64, s.o.), Sunderland, & William Smith (16/64, m.m.), Amble. William Smith (m.m.), Amble, became sole owner.

On 17 July 1865 the *Aaron Eaton* was sold to Luke Dyer, Robert Greenwell & John Hunter, all of Bishopwearmouth. They were succeeded by the following North-East Coast owners:

7.12.1870: Robert Greenwell, Sunderland.
8.7.1871: John William Hunter, Sunderland, acquired 44/64ths.
1877: John Mackenzie, Blyth.

A collier, she went ashore off Southend on 17 November 1873 but was later pulled clear by a couple of tugs which took her to London.

On 31 March 1877, while on passage from Blyth towards Karlscrona, Sweden, the *Aaron Eaton* (Capt. E. Todd) ran into a severe gale off the Norwegian coast. In a blinding shower of snow she was driven ashore and became a total wreck. Her crew were saved. She was the sixth vessel belonging to her Blyth owner to be lost in twelve months. All were well found and none were insured.

2   **ADVENTURE** (1837-1857)
Schooner   80 tons   57 x 16 x 10 ·2 feet
1828: Built Arbroath.
P/R: Dundee (1828/14)
Owners. *1.2.1837:* Registered at Alnmouth after being purchased for £615 by Henry George Gibb (16/64, m.m.), Henry Hindmarsh (16/64, blacksmith) & Margaret Simpson (16/64, widow), all Alnmouth; George Lilburn (16/64, King's messenger), London.
Master. *1.2.1837:* Henry Gibb.

In her twenty year career as an Alnmouth ship, the *Adventure* voyaged extensively around the British Isles and into the Baltic during the summer months. Calls were made at many Scotch ports, also to the Welsh ports of Bangor and Beaumaris from where she probably brought tiles back to her home port.

During April 1857 she was sold to John Walker, a Glasgow shipbuilder, following the death of Henry George Gibb.

3   **AGENORIA** (1861-1882)   O/N 29726
Snow   176 tons   95·3 x 23·3 x 12·7 feet
1861: Built Amble by Sanderson & Leighton.
Owners: *20.11.1861:* Isabella Sanderson (spinster) & Thomas Leighton (s.b., jointly 12/64), both Amble; James Shotton (11/64, s.o.), James Calder (11/64, contractor), Robert Green (10/64, agent), & John Shotton (8/64, m.t.), all Warkworth; Thomas Ditchburn (8/64, gardener), Knotley, Kent, & John Dryden (4/64, architect), Newcastle. *30.11.1868:* Robert Green transferred 10/64 ths to Donald McInnes (m.t.), Amble. *31.5.1873 share distribution:* James Calder (24/64), Thomas Ditchburn (8/64) & Robert Hardie (32/64, m.m.) Amble.

During 1869, when bound from Riga towards Fisherrow with hemp, the *Agenoria* put into the Forth. A contemporary newspaper report noted: "Feared to have suffered in gale of 14 June." Here are some examples of her later passages:

1870 Amble (sailed 22 November) to Lisbon. Capt. Robinson.
1872 Amble (sailed 8 August) to Lubeck. Capt. Robinson.
1878 Amble (sailed 5 August) to Norrkoping. Capt. Hardie.
1878 Amble (sailed 22 February) to Caen. Capt. Hardie.

Her British register was cancelled on 25 September 1882 when sold to A. Johnson, Stavanger, Norway. The 1888 *Lloyd's Register* has the endorsement "lost" against her name.

4   **AID**   O/N 22391
Brig   189 tons   76·6 x 20·3 x 13·5 feet
1841: Built Warkworth by George Surtees.
Owners: *23.3.1841:* George Wilkin (56/64, s.o.) & William Surtees (8/64, m.m.), both Monkwearmouth. *9.4.1846:* William Shepherd (48/64, s.o.) & Robert Bell (16/64, s.w.), both Blyth.

The *Aid* was wrecked on the Dutch coast on 14 September 1869.

5   **AILSA CRAIG** (1871-1880)   O/N 45591
Barque   467 tons   133·8 x 28·7 x 17·8 feet
23.11.1862: Launched at South Shields by Thomas Young & Co.
Owners. *11.12.1862:* Emmanuel Young (42/64) & Charles Octavius Young (22/64), both North Shields. *27.8.1868:* Shallet Hewson (s.o.), North Shields. *12.6.1871:* Shallet Hewson died. *2.10.1871:* John Marshall Henderson (13/64, s.o.), Amble; Thomas Collison (13/64, teacher), Alnwick; George Laing Scott (13/64, m.f.), Acklington; John Miller Dickson Patterson (13/64, sailmaker), Berwick; Richard Duffield (12/64, wine merchant), London. *28.4.1873:* Duffield transferred his 6/64ths to Patterson.

On what was her maiden voyage, the *Ailsa Craig* went from the Tyne to Aden which was reached on 3 May 1863. She had a troublesome voyage in 1867/68 after leaving Foochow for New York on 12 December. It was next reported that she had put into Singapore "in distress" and was to unload for repairs.

On 23 February 1874, when Amble/Alnwick owned, the *Ailsa Craig* left the Tyne for Bahia. Two days later, when struggling in heavy weather off the Shetland Islands, her masts went by the board. At the same time fire broke out in the fo'c'sle destroying much of the crews clothing. Lying in this disabled condition several ships were requested to take her in tow all refused until the Norwegian steamer *Leif* came along. Aberdeen was reached on 15 March.

With the exception of George Laing Scott, all of the owners transferred their shares to James Brown, a London master mariner, on 19 February 1880. Her local Custom House Register was closed on 2 October on transfer to the capital. Her name had disappeared from *Lloyd's Register* by 1885.

6   **ALNWICK CASTLE** (1842-1848)
Schooner   54 tons   58·5 x 15·4 feet
1842: Built Aberdeen by Alexander Hall & Sons. Cost £700.
Owners. *28.9.1842:* Robert Simpson (21/64, ship agent) & George Potter (21/64, m.m.), both Alnmouth; Edward Thew (22/64, m.t.), Alnwick.
Masters. *28.9.1842:* George Potter. *21.5.1854:* John Emmerson.

Built by a firm which were later to construct some of the finest tea clippers, the *Alnwick Castle* was transferred to Clay registration on 25 May 1848

7   *ALNWICK PACKET*   (?1824-1825)
Schooner   103 tons   67·4 x 19·4 x 9·1 feet
1802: Built Berwick.
P/R: Berwick (1812/9)
Owners. *7.10.1824:* John Appleby (corn factor), Low Buston.
Master. *7.10.1824:* William Moor.
    During November 1825 the *Alnwick Packet* was lost when on passage from London to Alemouth.

8   *ALNWICK PACKET*   (1838-1841)   O/N 16722
Schooner-brig   99 tons   65·6 x 18·6 x 11·3 feet
1838: Built Blyth by William Shepherd.
Owners. *23.2.1838:* Edward Thew (21/64, s.o.), Alnwick; John Appleby (21/64, corn merchant), Buston; Joseph Hodgson (22/64, s.o.), Blyth.
Master. *23.2.1838:* William Crossman. *2.3.1838:* Thomas Rochester.
    On 1 June 1841 the *Alnwick Packet* was acquired by Joseph Hodgson, a Blyth shipowner. He mortgaged her to John Brown of Seaton Sluice "as security for debt" on 2 October 1854. She was later transferred to the London registration after acquisition by Thomas Weddon of 15, Great St Helens, London.

9   *AMBLE*   (1857-1878)   O/N 18700
Snow   !42 tons   86·9 x 21·7 x 12·2 feet
1857: Built Amble, probably by James Sanderson & Thomas Leighton.
Owners: *27.4.1857:* James Smith (16/64, m.m.), Isabella Sanderson (12/64, spinster), James Sanderson (10/64, s.b.) & Thomas Leighton (10/64, s.b.), all Amble; John Dryden (16/64, s.o.), Newcastle. *21.6.1859:* James Sanderson died. *23.1.1863 share distribution:* John Dryden (16/64), Isabella Sanderson (30/64) & Thomas Leighton (18/64).
    A Baltic trader in her early days. In 1863 she made a 45 day passage between Cronstadt and Coquet Roads under a Capt. Wilson. In the following year she arrived off the Tyne on 16 June - 18 days out from Memel with a cargo of deals.
    During 1870 she made at least seven round voyages between Amble and Boulogne and one to Calais under the command of J. Wandless. In the following year a call was made at Lubeck.
    On 11 February 1878, the *Amble's* register was closed following her conversion to a lighter.

10   *AMITY*   (1846)
Sloop   51 tons   51·5 x 16·2 x 7·9 feet
1.2.1811: Taken as a prize by H.M.Cutter *Favourite* and condemned by the High Court of Admiralty.
P/R: Arbroath (1845/29).
Owners. *18.3.1846:* Thomas Browne (s.o.), Amble.
Master. *18.3.1846:* Robert Gordon Young.
    The *Amity* did not remain an Amble ship for very long. On 9 September 1846 - six months after being acquired - she was sold to Hugh Watkins, a master mariner of Llanarvoy, Carnarvon. E. Jones was appointed master. She was transferred to the Pwllheli register on 12 January 1847.

11   *AMPHITRITE* (1884-1891)   O/N 2201
Snow   214 tons   80 x 24·9 feet
1776: Built North Shields.
1802: New bottom, decks and upperworks.
1807: New bottom and damage repairs.
1820: Thoroughly repaired at Howdon Dock.
Owners. *12.10.1786:* Shallett Dale (m.m.), Thomas Allen (m.t.), William Addison (tallow chandler) & others, all of Newcastle. *19.7.1802:* Shallet Dale, Arthur Donkin (block & mast maker), Francis & Thomas Hurry, Ann Kirkley (widow), & William Linskill, all North Shields; Ralph Clarke, London; John Gaul Harrison, South Shields; Francis & Thomas Hurry, shipbuilders, Howdon; *9.3.1805:* Joseph Elder (s.o.), & Mary Elder (widow), both North Shields; William Linskill, Tynemouth; Ralph Clarke (coal factor), London. *21.9.1820:* Francis & Thomas Hurry & Ann Kirkley no longer had an interest in the vessel. *20.3.1848:* Robert Laing (22/64), John Laing (21/64), & Charles Laing (21/64), all North Shields ship-owners. *3.6.1862:* William Davison (s.o.), North Shields. *14.5.1872:* James Young (s.o.), South Shields. *12.12.1884:* Hugh Andrews (colliery owner), Swarland, Northumberland.

The *Amphitrite* was 108 years old when Hugh Andrews acquired her! She probably had the longest life of any Tyne built sailing ship. Hugh Andrews leased her to Joseph Leask & Company of Lerwick for use as a coal hulk in 1885. She continued in that lowly role until wrecked off Portland on 11 November 1891. In a letter to the Registrar of Shipping, a repre-sentative of the Channel Coaling Company (by whom she was either owned or leased) wrote: "....if she could ever be raised, it would be only for the copper which is on her and would be no further use to us." An unworthy epitaph for a ship of such antiquity.

12   *ASHBY* (1861-1863)
Brigantine   168 tons   94·2 x 23·8 x 11·2 feet
1854: Built Granville, Nova Scotia.
P/R: St John, New Brunswick.
Owners: *? date:* Aaron Eaton, Saint John, N.B. *29.6.1861:* James Smith (s.o.), Amble.

The *Ashby* was wrecked on a reef off Pirangi, about six leagues south of Rio Grande do Norte, on the coast of Brazil, on 22 August 1863. She had been bound from Lisbon towards Rio de Janeiro.

13   *AULD REEKIE* (1865-1875)   O/N 43994
Schooner   192 tons   101·4 x 21·9 x 13·4 feet
1861: Built Grangemouth by Adamson.
P/R: London (1862/17).
Owners: *19.6.1865:* John Marshall Henderson (22/64, s.o.), Walter Thoburn (16/64, builder), George Mason (16/64, m.t.) & Roger Dawson (10/64, m.m.), all Amble. *25.9.1868:* George Mason died. *25.9.1865:* Dawson sold his 10/64ths to George Simpson (fisherman), Hauxley.

The *Auld Reekie* was sold to Samuel Alexander Sadler, a Middlesbrough manufacturing chemist, on 20 April 1875, and transferred to that port.

14   *AYDON FOREST* (1874-1887)   O/N 70390
Barque   500 tons   147·3 x 30·2 x 18·1 feet
1874: Built Sunderland by James Gardner.
Owners. *18.11.1874:* William (15/64, m.o.,s.o.), Isabella (2/64, spinster) & Robert (2/64, s.o.) Davison, William Turnbull (5/64, m.t.), Peter Egdington (5/64, miller), Abel Scholfield (4/64, s.o.), Henry Spittle (4/64, baker), Joseph Coxon (2/64, woodman), & George Thomp-

son (4/64, plumber), all Alnwick; John Wilson (4/64, builder) & Thomas Shine (3/64, mining engineer), both Lesbury; John Wood (2/64, colliery owner) & John Wilkinson Arnett (3/64, farmer), both Wigham; Henry McCauler (3/64, m.m.), North Shields; James Gardner (4/64, s.b.), Sunderland; John Smith (2/64, tailor), Newcastle. *4.1.1887 share distribution:* William (19/64), Isabella (2/64), Robert (5/64), John (2/64) & George (1/64) Davison, William Turnbull (15/64, m.t.), Peter Egdington (5/64), Henry Spittle (4/64), Claringa Lydia Gatley (2/64) & Michael Storley Friers (2/64), all Alnwick; John Wood (3/64) & John Wilkinson Arnett (3/63), Wigham; John Wilson (4/64), Lesbury; John Smith (4/64), Newcastle.

The *Aydon Forest* tramped the world seeking profitable freights. Here are some of her wanderings:

1877	Glasgow to Montevideo (arrived prior to 20 Nov.)
1878	Rangoon (sailed 11 April) to Falmouth.
	Sunderland (sailed 17 Sept.) to Padang. (Capt. Galle)

She left Padang for Batavia (Djakarta) in February 1879, went aground near the latter port but was re-floated and repaired.

1880	Samarang to Queenstown 132 days.
	(13 April: spoken off Cape of Good Hope by steamer *Venice*)
	Havre to Miramichi 42 days. (Capt. John May)
	Miramichi to Ayr (arrived 24 October)
1880/81	Gravesend to Montevideo.
1881	Montevideo to Rangoon 61 days.
	Rangoon to Falmouth 130 days.
	Falmouth to Amsterdam 9 days.
1881/82	Ymuiden to Sourabaya (Surabaja) 110 days. (Capt. John May)
1882	Cheribon (Tjirebon) to Melbourne.
	Melbourne to Newcastle N.S.W. (18 Aug: arrived)
	Newcastle N.S.W. to Banjowahjie (? Banjuwangi)
	Banjowahjie to Batavia (Djakarta)
1883	Java to Melbourne.
	Swatow to Queenstown (Cobh).
1884	Cardiff to Cheribon 115 days. (Capt. J. P. Trail)
	Cheribon to Sourabaya 9 days.
	Sourabaya (20 Sept: sailed) to Lisbon.
	Lisbon to Liverpool .
1885	Liverpool to Troon (17 January: arrived)
	(rough passage)
	Troon to Demerara 48 days.
	Demerara to Mobile (18 May: arrived)
	Mobile to Calais (13 August: arrived.)
1885/86	Grangemouth to Buenos Ayres 65 days.
	(heavy weather passage - lost boats)
1886	Buenos Ayres to Pensacola 38 days.
	(slow passage)

The *Aydon Forest* (Capt. John P. Trail) went missing after leaving Mobile on 20 July 1887 bound towards Havre.

---

15   ***BONNE MERE*** (1866-1874)   O/N 53477
Smack   29 tons   47·1 x 17·3 x 7·5 feet
1858: Built Boulogne Sur Mer, France.
Owners. *4.8.1866*: Thomas Scott (s.o.), Warkworth. *5.4.1867:* Thomas Scott died.

20.9.1867: John Henderson (m.t.), Hauxley.

This French built vessel kept her Gallic name when Thomas Scott bought her. During October 1870, after a six month lay up, the *Bonne Mere* carried a cargo of timber from Amble to Alnmouth, under the command of Capt. Henderson. She is reported to have been: "lost in Warkworth Harbour and broken up in 1874."

16   **BREEZE** (1841-1845)
Schooner   136 tons   70·1 x 20 x 11·8 feet
1839: Built Warkworth Harbour by George Surtees.
Owners. *29.7.1839:* George Hudson (16/64, s.o.), William Kirkwood (16/64, s.o.), & William Surtees (16/64, s.o.), all Monkwearmouth; George Surtees (16/64, s.o.), late of Monkwearmouth (he had moved to Amble, at least while the *Breeze* was being built). *2.2.1841:* Luke & William Hindmarch (32/64ths each), both Alnwick merchants. *27.2.1843:* Luke Hindmarch became sole owner.
Masters: *29.7.1839:* William Kirkwood. *30.7.1839:* James Campbell. *5.2.1841:* John Asplin. *17.8.1846:* John Lindsay.

The *Breeze* was sold to William Edgley (s.o.) and Daniel Ellund (grocer), both of Hartlepool, on 14 February 1848. Ellund became sole owner on 5 June 1852. She was re-registered at Colchester on 22 February 1853.

17   **BRITANNIA** (1833-1842)
Sloop   51 tons   47 x 16 feet
1822: Built Barrowstones.
P/R: Dunbar (*20.1.1826*)
Owners. *19.11.1833:* Henry Hindmarsh (32/64, blacksmith) & Edward Gibb (32/64, m.m.), both Alnmouth.
Masters. *19.11.1833:* Henry Gibb. *28.10.1836:* Robert Bain. *14.4.1841:* Robert Richardson. *22.4.1842:* Lawrence Sharp. *1.10.1842:* Robert McIntern.

One of the smaller coasters, the *Britannia* made many voyages to ports on the East Coast of Scotland and occasionally went further afield to Dublin and the Welsh slate ports. On 21 January 1836 she sustained considerable stem and bottom damage after grounding on the Pan Bush Shoal, near Coquet Island, and had to be towed into Amble for temporary repairs.

On 26 November 1842 the *Britannia* was transferred to Dunbar.

18   **CAMPERDOWN** (? -1883)   O/N 23436
Barque   946 tons   153 x 35·3 x 24 feet (L/R)
1847: Built Sunderland by J. Laing.
Registered in London.
Owners. *1847:* Duncan Dunbar, London. *1883 L/R:* Hugh Andrews (coal owner), 25, Queen Street, Newcastle - this was Andrew's business address.

Frigate built for the Indian trade, the *Camperdown* made many voyages out east in her early days when owned by Duncan Dunbar, a famous London shipowner. In 1853 a passage was made from Cork to the Sandheads (Calcutta) in 101 days. On 5 October 1864, although driven ashore, she survived a devastating cyclone which did so much damage to shipping lying at Calcutta .

On 11 April 1883 the *Camperdown* left the Tyne for Barbados with 1,300 tons of coal. Six days later she put into Dartmouth making water. Seven hundred tons of coal had to be discharged. The voyage to Barbados was abandoned. From Dartmouth she went across to Sydney, Cape Breton, in 37 days with 600 tons of coal. A cargo of deals was loaded at

Sydney for Denia, Spain. When ten days out she collided with the steamer *Iowa* and sustained damage to the starboard bow and lost her head gear. She put back into Sydney where she was sold at public auction on 29 September. Hull and spars fetched $2,700; stores $1,000. Later a court case was brought by the chief officer, George Cowie, and the bosun, William Hedley Young, for wages not paid between 17 October 1883 and 4 January 1884 - the date they arrived back in the United Kingdom. The owner claimed that the *Camperdown* had been wrecked, therefore wages would cease. The court decided that she had been sold and supported the men's claim. The chief officer's pay was £6 a month.

Despite being ignominiously sold at auction and described as a "wreck" the *Camperdown* survived for another four years under the ownership of A. Haley of Sydney, Cape Breton, before being condemned.

19   *CAMPSIE GLEN* (1874-1888)   O/N 70381
Barque   490 tons   145·4 x 30 x 17·9 feet
1874: Built Sunderland by James Gardner.
Owners. *16.7.1874:* William (12/64, s.o.), Robert (12/64, s.o.) & George (4/64,s.o.) Davison, David Mackenley sen. (14/64, s.o.), Henry Spittle (8/64, baker), Duncan Smith (8/64, m.m.) & George Simpson (6/64, chemist), all Alnwick.

The maiden voyage of the *Campsie Glen* took her out to Burma under the command of Duncan Smith. She left Rangoon for her return passage to the United Kingdom on 6 March 1875.

The year 1880 was a bad one for the ship and her master. When homeward bound from Swatow she put into St Helena on 7 July to bury the body of Capt. Smith's son who had died four days earlier. Falmouth was eventually reached on 1 September at the end of a long, 155 day passage from the Chinese port. From Falmouth she went up to Greenock in 7 days. After 45 days discharging and loading the *Campsie Glen* set out for Montevideo. Soon after sailing Capt. Smith was knocked insensible by a heavy sea which swept the decks. A call was made at Passage East (Waterford Harbour) for medical assistance and repairs. It appears that Capt. Smith was relieved by Capt. John Trail at this time. Montevideo was reached on 27 January. Here are some of her subsequent passages:

1881	Buenos Ayres (8 March: sailed) to Rangoon.	
	Rangoon to New York.	
1881/82	New York to Timaru, New Zealand 95 days.	
1882	Newcastle N.S.W. to Sourabaya.	
	Sourabaya to Melbourne (10 October: arrived)	
	Newcastle N.S.W. to Sourabaya (Dec: arrived)	

On 13 May 1883 it was reported that she had left Madras to: "load on the coast for London."

1884	Buenos Ayres to Cape Haytien 37 days (Capt. Henderson)	
	Fort Liberte to Havre 37 days.	
	Havre to Cardiff (24 Oct: arrived) 4 days.	
	Cardiff to Zanzibar (2 March: arrived)	
	(made a call at Delgoa Bay)	
1886	Tyne (2 Feb: sailed) to Buenos Ayres.	

In a letter dated 25 August 1888 William Davison, her managing owner, wrote to the Registrar of Shipping: "The *Campsie Glen* put into Rio Janeiro dismasted and was surveyed - found cost of repairs was more than the vessel would be worth and therefore was abandoned". Her register had been closed ten days earlier and endorsed "condemned".

20   *CASPIAN*
            199 tons   81 x 23·5 x 13·5 feet
1849: Built Sunderland by Lister & Bartram.
Owners: Listed in *Amble & District* by T.L. McAndrews as belonging to J.H. Barrie, Amble.
1856 L/R: Dotchin & Co., Whitby *1860 L/R:* Barry & Co., Whitby. .
Master: *? date:* Dichburn.
The *Caspian* was no longer listed in *Lloyd's Register* after 1870.

21   *CEDAR* (1858-1888)   O/N 21068
Brig   218 tons   98·9 x 25·1 x 14·4 feet
1858: Built Sunderland by W. Briggs (J.M. Reed has also been described as the builder).
1884/85: Deck-house and round-house added increasing registered tonnage to 225.
Owners: *23.3.1858:* George & Robert Richardson (16/64 each, both builders), Andrew
Richardson (16/64, draper), all Amble; Thomas Richards (16/64, m.m.), Shoreham.
21.2.1868: Andrew Richardson transferred 8/64ths to William Richardson (medical student),
Amble. *20.11.1872:* Thomas Richards transferred 8/64ths to Maria Richards (spinster),
Amble. *20.5.1875:* Maria Richards transferred her 8/64ths to John Fish (United Methodist
Minister), Brigg, Lincoln. *16.8.1876:* Robert Richardson transferred his 16/64ths to Andrew
Richardson. *17.5.1881:* Thomas Richards died. *13.2.1885   share distribution:* George
Richardson (16/64), Andrew Richardson (24/64), Executors of Thomas Richards (16/64) &
William Richardson (8/64).
       During 1871 the *Cedar* (Capt. Chesney) made a passage from London to Amble and
then to Malmo.
       On 23 April 1888 she was sold to C. Nielson, Laurvig (?Larvik) and re-named *Alma*.
He was followed in 1893 by P. Mekkelsen of Brevig; 1897 by S.C. Larsen, Brevig, and two
years later by S. Abrahamsen, belonging to the same port. She was sold for breaking up at
Calais in February 1902.

22   *CERES*
A vessel of this name is listed in *Amble and District* by T.L. McAndrews as belonging to
Hugh Andrews. Unable to trace.

23   *CEYLON* (1866-1870)   O/N 53459
Snow   240 tons   103 x 25·2 x 14·7 feet
1866: Built Pallion, Sunderland, by Robinson.
1867: Woman's bust figurehead fitted.
Owners. *12.4.1866:* John Henry Barry (34/64, s.o.), John Fennell Holdsworth (10/64, s.o.) &
Edward Whitfield (coal fitter), all Amble; Nicholas Wood (8/64, farmer) & James Thompson
(4/64, draper), both Felton.
       On 18 April 1870 the *Ceylon* was run down and sunk eight miles south -south-east of
the Newarp Light Vessel (positioned off Winterton, Norfolk) in dense fog by the French
steamer *Ernestine*. Both ships were proceeding at a little over three knots. The *Ceylon* was
bound from Blyth to Port Said with coal, the *Ernestine* from Dieppe to Grimsby.

24   *CEYLON* (1870-1881)   O/N 60551
Barque   399 tons   29·5 x 28·5 x 17·3 feet
1870: Built Hylton, Sunderland, by George Bartram.
Owners. *8.6.1870:* John Henry Barry (32/64), Edward Whitfield (8/64) & John Fennell
Holdsworth (6/64), all Amble; Henry Thomas Dixon (3/64), Blyth; Nicholas Wood (8/64) &
James Thompson (4/64) both Felton; John Claxton (3/64), Whitby. *8.12.1870:* Holdsworth

transferred his 6/64ths to Barry. *17.1.1874:* Thompson transferred his 4/64ths to Barry. All were described as shipowners.

The *Ceylon* was built for the Mediterranean and West Indian trades. Her British Registration was closed on 3 June 1881 following purchase by M.N. Rodinis of Leghorn, Italy, who re-named her *Matteo Nicola.* Three years later she is listed as the *Matteo R.* and by 1889 *Lloyd's* describes her as the *Matteo R ex Matteo Nicola ex Ivancich ex Ceylon* belonging to Giuseppe Zacevich, of Lussinpiccolo (Mali Losinj), in what was then Austria. Her name was again changed, this time to *Esperance,* when acquired by J. Mirio of Bordeaux in 1894. She went missing, when on passage towards Miquelon, after leaving Arzew, Algeria, on 18 March 1897.

25   *CHALURANGA* (1871)   O/N 29257
Barque   334 tons   115·2 x 27·3 x 16·7 feet
1861: Built Sunderland by J.J. Brown.
Owners. *27.2.1861:* Ralph Milbanks Hudson (16/64), John Candlish (16/64) & George Winlow Hudson (12/64), all Sunderland; Thomas Scott (12/64) & Richard White Cousens (8/64), both London. All shipowners. *28.2.1871:* William Edward Melrose (16/64, s.o.), Robert Richardson (16/64, s.o.) & Jane Alice Richardson (16/64, spinster), all Amble; William Henry Schollar (16/64, s.o.), Blyth.

The *Chaluranga's* career as an Amble ship lasted for less than six months. On 26 August 1871 she was lost on the Nickmans Ground, off Dago Island, Estonia.

26   *CHARLES MOLLEY* (1845-1853)   O/N 4695
Brig   215 tons
1845: Built Low Southwick, Sunderland, by William Petrie.
Owners. *8.12.1845:* Thomas Browne, Amble   *21.8.1848:* Elizabeth Browne (spinster), Amble House.
Masters. *22.8.1853:* James Straker. *6.2.1846:* George Liddle.

On 22 August 1853 the *Chas Molley* was transferred to Cape Town registration. By the 1880's she was back in the United Kingdom under the ownership of J.T. Smith, London. She was lost during the years 1885/1886.

27   *CHRISTINA MURRAY* (1845-1848)
Brig   185 tons   79·1 x 21·9 x 12·9 feet
1845: Built Sunderland by Todd & Brown.
Owners. *3.1.1845:* Thomas Browne (56/64), Amble House, Warkworth, & William Robson (8/64, m.m.), North Shields. *31.7.1846:* Thomas Browne became sole owner.
Masters: *3.1.1845:* William Robson *1.8.1846:* George Marr. *16.11.1846:* William Cooper.
The *Christina Murray* was transferred to Alloa on 11 July 1848.

28   *CLEVELAND*
The *Newcastle Journal* of 21 July 1862 described this vessel as the *Cleveland* "of Warkworth" and went on to report that she had been badly damaged following a collision with the French brigantine *Amazone,* near Cromer Rock Buoy, on 18 April. A subsequent Admiralty Court found the French ship soley to blame.

29   *CORAL ISLE* (1871-1873)   O/N 29692
Barque   281 tons   106·4 x 26·3 x 16·5 feet
1861: Built Hylton, Sunderland, by W. Naizby.
1875: Re-rigged as snow.

P/R: Scarborough (1861/8)

Owners. *9.7.1869:* Samuel Peter Austin (s.b.), Sunderland. *19.7.1869:* James Heatley (s.o.), Blyth. *20.7.1869:* Heatley transferred 16/64ths each to Robert Simpson (commercial traveller), London; George Potter (m.m.) & Ann Simpson (widow), both Alnmouth. *20.3.1871:* Heatley transferred 8/64ths to Matthew George Simpson (agent), Alnmouth.

On 15 July 1875 the *Coral Isle* (Capt. Andrew Heatley) was wrecked at Filsand, near Riga, when on passage from Cronstadt towards the United Kingdom.

30   *CORAL QUEEN* (1866-1872)   O/N 4597

Barque   241 tons   115·8 x 24·4 x 14·7 feet

1854: Built Pallion, Sunderland, by E. Bailey.

P/R: London (1854/468).

Owners. *16.5.1866:* Sold by Milhush & Co., London, to John Henderson (13/64, gas manufacturer), John Henry Gibb (8/64, m.m.), Ann Elizabeth Sanderson (4/64, spinster) & Thomas Leighton (4/64, s.b.), all Amble; Benjamin Pope (13/64, m.t.), Alnwick; Matthew Thompson (13/64, grocer) & Thomas Wardle (9/64, butcher), both Warkworth.

On 2 August 1866, when off St Abbs Head, the *Coral Queen* was struck by a heavy sea. Three of the gudgeons, which secured the rudder, broke. The rudder was secured by chains but two days later these broke and the rudder was lost. Nevertheless the disabled ship was able to reach the Tyne. In the following year a slow, 48 day passage was made from the Tyne to Lisbon.

The *Coral Queen* (Capt. Curry) was wrecked at Niddingen, near Gothenburg, on 20 November 1872. Sir Walter Runciman in his *Collier Brigs and their Sailors* describes her as: "A smart little vessel" and Capt. Curry as: "one of the most experienced and capable captains".

31   *CROFT* (1836-1843)

Schooner   63 tons   52·3 x 16·9 feet

1835: Built Cowpen Quay, Blyth, by George Bowman & Thomas Drummond.

Owners. *22.4.1835:* Bowman & Drummond (32/64 each), Blyth shipbuilders. *25.1.1836:* John Herdsman (doctor of medicine), Lesbury, acquired 63/63ths. *14.3.1836:* Transferred to Berwick registration. Conrad Thew (24/64, m.t.), Alnwick; Robert Simpson (22/64, wharfinger) & George Potter (21/64, m.m.), both Alnmouth.

In 1839 the *Croft* was listed as a regular trader between the Tyne and Alnmouth with George Potter as master. She foundered on 23 April 1843 when on passage from Grangemouth to Berwick.

32   *CUBA* (1876)   O/N 947

Schooner   137 tons   77·7 x 21·6 x 13·3 feet

1839: Built Port Glasgow.

Registered at London.

Owners. *1875 L/R:* E.P. Smith, London. *Circa 1876*: H. Andrews, Amble.

During February 1876 the *Cuba* (Capt. J. Sheriff) took coal from Amble to Rouen. Later the same year she came from Bremerhaven to Amble and left, on 2 October, for Dundee. Her name was deleted from *Lloyd's Register* the following year.

33   *DERWENTWATER* (1856-1868)   O/N 14502

Brig   171 tons   86·4 x 23·7 x 12·9 feet

1856: Built Tyne Main by Gaddy & Lamb.

Owners. *15.4.1856:* John Harrison (32/64), Ratcliffe Colliery; Carl Lange (8/64) & Joseph

Harrison (24/64), both Newcastle merchants. *1.7.1861:* Lange transferred his 8/64ths to Joseph Harrison. At about this time Joseph Harrison was described as a colliery owner of Amble. *23.9.1862:* Joseph Harrison became sole owner.

On 19 April 1856 the *Derwentwater* was towed from the Tyne to Amble, just after completion, to load for St Petersburg. She was one of the first North-East Coast ships sail for Russia at the termination of he Crimean War.

The *Derwentwater* struck the Scaw Reef, at the entrance to the Kattegat, and capsized on 1 December 1867. Her crew scrambled onto her bottom from where they were rescued by the *Westmorland* of Sunderland which brought them to Grimsby.

Early the following year the up-turned hull of the *Derwentwater* was found. An attempt was made to get her into Lysski (? Lysekil, near Uddevalla, Sweden) but she broke up during a gale. Her cargo, probably timber, was saved.

34 *DIAMOND* (1835-1845)

Sloop   66 tons   43·7 x 17·1 x 8·5 feet

1817: Built Blyth by John Davidson & Sons.

Owners. *16.5.1817:* Edward Poad jun., & Mary Poad (spinster), both Blyth. *19.12.1824:* Edward Poad jun.(48/64, mariner) & (m.m., held 16/64th's for his wife Mary [nee Mary Poad]) *14.10.1835:* Adam Smith (16/64) & Dennis Poad (48/64, administrator of Edward Poad, Alemouth), both Alemouth.

Masters. *16.5.1817:* William Poad. *10.10.1817:* Dennis Poad. *27.7.1820:* William Poad. *5.2.1821:* David Miller. *15.3.1833:* William Clarke. *3.4.1823:* Adam Smith. *26.8.1837:* Richard Reay. *25.4.1838:* William Poad. *10.8.1839:* John Anderson *19.10.1839:* James Glindining. *3.11.1849:* James Johnson.

The *Diamond* was acquired by George Lee, a Tweedmouth shipbuilder, on 2 April 1845. Five years later she was transferred to Aberdeen.

35 *DOROTHY* (1866-1879)   O/N 7400

Snow   345 tons   95 x 25·5 x 15·3 feet

1856: Built Sunderland by Hodgson & Gardner.

Owners. *26.7.1856:* James Walker (s.o.), Sunderland. *12.4.1866:* William Stephenson (13/64), William Stanton (13/64) & George John Stanton (12/64), all Alnmouth shipowners; Benjamin Pope (13/64, china merchant) & Abel Scholfield (13/64, s.o.), both Alnwick. *7.6.1870:* William Stanton died. *20.4.1877:* George John Stanton died. *7.4.1879:* Benjamin Pope died.

On 21 November 1879 the *Dorothy* was sold to James Knott of Newcastle, who, at the time, was described as a shipbroker. He later became a prominent shipowner and founder of the well known Prince Line. Under his ownership she made a number of voyages to the West Indies and Central America before being relegated to the coastal trade in later years.

Here are subsequent share holding and ownership changes: *7.4.1880:* Knott transferred 24/64ths to Christian Rudulph Fernando Thiedeman, & 8/64ths to James Miller (colliery agent), both Newcastle; and 8/64ths to Peter Moorson (m.m.), Robin Hood's Bay. *3.10.1887:* Knott transferred 2/64ths to William Milburn (m.o., ships husband), North Shields. *18.4.1888:* Knott transferred a further 2/64ths to William Milburn (m.o., ships husband), North Shields. *18.4.1888:* Thiedeman transferred his 24/64ths back to Knott. *12.8.1889:* John Elliott (m.o., grocer), Howdon. *10.9.1889:* Elliott transferred 16/64ths each to John Lee (butcher), Newcastle; William Milburn (ships husband), North Shields, & James Walker (m.m.), South Shields.

On 12 December 1892 the *Dorothy's* registration was cancelled following her conversion to a lighter.

36 *DOUSE* (1882-1889)   O/N 59653
Brigantine   195 tons   102·6 x 24 x 12·9 feet
1868: Built Mount Stewart, Prince Edward Island, by Douse.
P/R: Ardrossan (1874/2)
Owners. *1870 L/R:* J. Douse, Prince Edward Island. *1871 L/R:* Miller & Co.,Liverpool.
27.5.1882: Hugh Andrews (colliery proprietor), Warkworth Harbour. Eleven days before
John Park, also of Warkworth Harbour, had been appointed manager.

The *Douse* made a number of coal laden passages from Amble to Calais under the command of Robert Neesham.

On 21 December 1889 she was sold to Robert Taylor, a Dundee coal merchant, and
transferred to the Scotch port the following year. She returned to the North-East Coast on 1
June 1891 when John Wilkinson Lawes of South Shields acquired her. The *Douse* was
wrecked off the North Foreland on 13 January 1892.

37   *DOVE* (1861)   O/N 3767
Snow   213 tons   85·9 x 20·9 x 13·1 feet
1847: Built Pictou, Nova Scotia.
P/R: Liverpool (1847/261).
Owners: *? date:* Joseph Brown (s.b.), Liverpool. *9.1.1848:* Gilbert Henderson (43/64, s.o.)
& Robert Urwin (21/64, butcher), both Newcastle. *13.4.1848:* Robert Urwin became sole
owner *10.4.1852:* Gilbert Henderson (43/64) & Robert Urwin (21/64). *15.1.1853:* Thomas
Wilkin (flour dealer), Newcastle, acquired 21/64ths from Henderson. *11.1.1861:* Joseph
Harrison, Radcliffe; John Henderson, Hauxley; and Edward Thomas Simpson, Alnmouth.

On 3 January 1852, when Tyne owned, the *Dove* caught fire while lying in a Cardiff
drydock. It was supposed to have started in the cabin stove. With the aid of the town fire-
engine, the ship herself was saved. The master and his wife lost everything. During the following year her master, Cuthbert Parker, jumped overboard in a "fit of delirium" and was
drowned in the Black Sea on 8 November 1853.

The *Dove* had a short career as a Aln/Coquet ship; her register was transferred to London when acquired by John Hatehill Brenan on 15 September 1863,

38   *DUCHESS OF NORTHUMBERLAND* (1840-1843)
Schooner   65 tons   55·6 x 15·9 x 9·2 feet
1840: Built Amble by George Surtees.
Owner. *22.4.1841:* George Surtees (s.b.), Warkworth.
Masters. *22.4.1841*: George Surtees. *14.7.1842:* James Smith.

If the *Duchess of Northumberland's* Custom House Register is correct she is unique by
being built, owned and commanded by the same person - George Surtees!

On 21 June 1843 he sold her to James Garrow and James Smith of Montrose. She was
transferred to the Scotch port three weeks later

39   *EARL OF NEWBURGH* (1845-1848)
Brig   206 tons   83·6 x 21·9 x 14·1 feet
1845: Built Howdon Dock by Trotter & Young.
Owners. *24.4.1845:* Thomas Browne, Amble. *5.5.1845:* George Liddle, a Sunderland master
mariner acquired 4/64ths. *28.12.1847:* James Bainbridge, Lumley Thicks, Durham, acquired
4/64ths from Browne.
Masters. *24.4.1845:* George Liddle. *12.2.1846:* Andrew Davidson. *3.1.1849*: Robert Walton.

On 15 September 1848 the *Earl of Newburgh* was sold by the creditors of Thomas
Browne, her principle owner, to Robert Walton (22/64, m.m.) and John Rowantree (21/64,

s.o.), both of North Shields, and John Walton (21/64, painter), Middlesex. Robert Walton became sole owner on 9 December 1852.

She was lying at anchor in the Coquet Roads on 6 January 1854 when a terrific east-south-east gale blew up. Driven from her anchors, the coal laden *Earl of Newburgh* dragged ashore one mile south of Amble and became a total wreck. Eight other vessels were blown ashore in the same area by the same gale.

40 *EASTERN PROVINCE* (1874-1879)   O/N 21396

Barque   365 tons   125·5 x 27·2 feet
1858: Built Sunderland by Peverall & Davison.
P/R: Glasgow (1869/42).
Owners. *1867 L/R:* Falconer, London. *1871 L/R:* Singleton, Glasgow.: *15.6.1874:* John Henderson (s.o.), Amble. *1.7.1875:* Elizabeth Henderson (widow), Amble.

In her last year as an Amble ship, the *Eastern Province* made a passage from New Orleans to Rotterdam where she arrived on 28 April 1879 under the command of a Capt. Hodge. On 25 October she was sold to John Blumer Bushell, the South Shields shipbuilder.

The *Eastern Province's* British Registration was closed on 5 November 1880 after sale to H.T. Brandt of Copenhagen who renamed her *Felix Brandt.* She drops out of *Lloyd's Register* in 1888.

41 *ELBE* (1862-1863)   O/N 24415

Snow   211 tons   82·6 x 24·6 feet
1826: Built Sunderland by J. Storey.
P/R: London (1845/109).
Owners. *12.3.1846:* Henry Durham Stephenson (s.b.), Sunderland. *23.10.1846:* George Foster (s.o.), Monkwearmouth. *4.3.1854:* William Lisle (48/64), Seaham Harbour; William Matthews (16/64), Cullercoats. *9.11.1854:* Hannah Gibson (48/64, widow) & George Gibson Johnson (16/64, m.m.), both South Shields. *13.6.1862:* Robert Richardson (s.o.), Amble.

The *Elbe* was Amble owned for little more than four months before being sold to John Patterson, a Sunderland master mariner, on 6 October 1862. He had her until 23 November 1863 when it was reported that she had "foundered at sea".

42 *ELECTRA* (1882-1886)   O/N 50945

Brigantine   141 tons   96·4 x 23·1 x 12·1 feet
1864: Built Prince Edward Island by Duncan McRae.
Owners. *29.5.1882:* Hugh Andrews (colliery proprietor), Felton. *3.7.1882:* John Park, Warkworth Harbour, appointed managing owner.

Under the command of Robert Lewis, the *Electra* took cargoes of coal from Amble to Boulogne and Sheerness.

On 8 April 1886 her British Registration was closed following sale to French owners. No further trace.

43 *ELIZA LAING* (1873-1874)   O/N 28657

Barque   441 tons   127·9 x 28·6 x 18·8 feet
1862: Built Sunderland by D.A. Douglas.
P/R: Stockton (1862/7).
Owners. *23.12.1872:* Samuel Peter Austin (s.b.), Sunderland. *21.1.1873:* John Marshall Henderson (s.o.), Amble. *1.2.1873:* John James Fairbairn, Grizzlefield, Berwick, acquired 8/64ths; James Robert Laing, St Leonards, Sussex, 21/64ths, and John Miller Dickson Patterson, Berwick, 14/64ths.

On 13 March 1874 the *Eliza Laing* was wrecked on the Island of Sheik Shart (possibly Sheikh Shaib [Busheab] Island [26°48' N., 53°24'E.]), in the Persian (Arabian) Gulf.

44   **ELIZABETH** (1848-1862)   O/N 22859
Brig   234 tons   87·4 x 23 x 16 feet
1848: Built Sunderland by John Crown.
Owner. *9.5.1848:* Luke Hindmarsh (s.o.), Alnmouth.
Master. *9.5.1848:* James Moddrel.
During 1859, while loading at Odessa, the *Elizabeth* made so much water that her cargo had to be discharged. Her registration was transferred to Liverpool on 17 February 1862 when acquired by Hine & Co. The 1864/65 *Lloyd's Register* has the endorsement "lost" against her name.

45   **ELIZABETH HENDERSON** (1863-1873)   O/N 54606
Snow   98 tons   108·1 x 26·8 x 16·6 feet
1863: Built Sunderland by Hodgeson.
Owners: *7.5.1863:* John Henderson (48/64, s.o.), Amble, & Henry Gibb (16/64, m.m.), Alnmouth. *18.5.1872:* Henry Gibb transferred 8/64ths to Henry Heatley, an Alnwick draper.
During 1865 the *Elizabeth Henderson* made a 51 day passage from the Tyne to Naples. The Lizard had been passed 10 days out.
On 1 May 1873 she was wrecked off Paranagua, Brazil, when on passage from the Tyne towards Rio de Janeiro under the command of John Darling.

46   **EXPRESS** (?1825-1855)
Schooner   112 tons   64·6 x 21 x 10·6 feet
1816: "Captured at sea by some ship or vessel belonging to His Majesty and legally condemned and sold under order of the Court of Admiralty of Ireland (Berwick Custom House Register*)*."
Owners. *17.10.1825:* Edward Gibb (16/64, m.m. & administrator of George Gibb, Alemouth, deceased) & Thomas Annett (24/64, corn merchant), both Alnmouth; Charles Jacob Wilkinson (24/64, m.t.), London. *3.8.1830:* Gibb transferred his 16/64ths to John Appleby, Buston. *29.9.1840:* Following Appleby's death his 16/64ths were transferred to Edward Thew, Alnwick. *4.11.1846:* Edward Thew (40/64, m.t.), Alnwick, & Charles Jacob Wilkinson (24/64, m.t.), London. *26.1.1843:* Edward Thew transferred 8/64ths each to Robert Gibb (m.m.) & Robert Simpson (s.o.), both Alnmouth. *20.7.1843:* Following Wilkinson's death, his 24/64ths were transferred to Robert Young, London.
Master. *17.10.1825:* James Foster.
The *Express* spent much of her time on the Alnmouth to London trade, sometimes calling at Amble or Blyth for a coal cargo on the southward run. Her registration was transferred to London in 1855.

47   **FELIX LADBROKE** (1845)
Brig   205 tons   84·3 x 22 x 14·3 feet
1845: Built Cox Green, Sunderland, by Sykes Talbot & Sykes.
Owners. *4.3.1845:* Thomas Browne (coal owner), Amble. Soon after 8/64ths were transferred to Joseph Watson (m.m.), Sunderland. *4.7.1845:* Thomas Browne again became sole owner.
Masters. *4.3.1845:* Joseph Watson. *31.7.1845:* George Holmes.
The *Felix Ladbroke* had a very short career. She was lost on the Yorkshire coast during August 1845 - just about six months after her completion.

The *Express* lying at Black Eagle Wharf, Wapping, in 1856, the year after her registration had been transferred to London, but the name Alnmouth can still be seen on her stern. She has her top-sails loosely set for drying. On the left of the picture lies a coastal sloop, its square topsail in a neat "harbour stow." Alongside her is a Thames barge. The lighters full of barrels and the watermen's skiffs complete this evocative picture which captures so much of the atmosphere of a riverside wharf in the heyday of sail.

(Courtesy Museum in Dockland, PLA Collection)

48   FRANCES WESTERN (1845-1848)
Snow   169 tons   79·3 x 19·5 x 16·4 feet
1844: Built Friars Goose, Gateshead.
Owners. *11.1.1845:* Thomas Browne (56/64), Amble, & John Frederick (8/64, m.m.),
Monkwearmouth.
Master: *11.1.1845:* John Frederick.
    The *Frances Western's* register was closed on 24 May 1848 and endorsed: "lost per
declaration of master".

49   FRIENDSHIP (1875-1886)   O/N 3483
Snow   267 tons   95 x 25·9 feet
17.12.1807: Condemned as a prize by the High Court of Admiralty after being taken from
the Danes, prior to hostilities, by H.M. Sloop *Railleur* (V.Collard, commander).
Owners. *9.11.1833:* Thomas Barker (s.o.), South Shields. *1.12.1870:* Christopher Dove
Barker (32/64, banker), Geat Malvern, Worcester, & Thomas Bell Barker (32/64, s.o.), South
Shields). *11.1875:* Hugh Andrews (colliery owner), place of abode given as Newcastle.
    The *Friendship's* register was cancelled on 25 March 1886 and endorsed "broken up".

50   GALILEE (1866-1874)   O/N 53474
Snow   247 tons   103·6 x 25·4 x 14·7 feet
1866: Built Sunderland by Richard Thompson.
Owners. *17.7.1866:* George Richardson (16/64) & William Wood (8/64, m.m.), both Amble;
Robert Davison (16/64), David McKenly (16/64) & William Davison (8/64), all Alnwick
shipowners. *21.2.1870:* George Richardson died *27.12.1873:* George Richardson's 16/64ths
transferred to George Simpson (chemist), Alnwick.
    On 23 January 1874 the *Galilee* stranded and became a total loss in the French West
Indies.

51   GAMBIER (1835-1837)
ex *Laboureux*
11.7.1807: Condemned as a prize by the High Court of Admiralty after being captured from
the French by the British 5th Rate *Pomone* (Robert Barrie, commander).
P/R: at Sandwich (17.5.1832).
Owners. *16.5.1835:* Sold by L. Hale, Broadstairs, to Joseph Hodgeson, Crofton Mill, Northumberland. *11.10.1835:* Hodgeson transferred 21/64ths each to John Appleby (corn merchant), Buston, & Edward Thew (m.t.), Alnwick.
Master. *14.7.1835:* Henry Heatley.
    The *Gambier* (Capt. Hedley) was wrecked near the Humber on 22 May 1837.

52   GARIBALDI (1869-1872)
Smack   36 tons   53·5 x 16·6 x 7·8 feet
1861: Built Fraserburgh.
P/R: Kirkwall (1861/1).
Owners. *18.6.1869:* John Henderson (m.t.), Amble. *20.4.1870:* James Henderson (m.m.),
Amble.
    Here are some passages made by the *Garibaldi:*
                    1870   Sunderland to Amble (Capt. H. Nicholls)
                           Amble to Dingwall
                           North Sunderland to Amble (barrels)
                           Amble to North Sunderland (herrings)

1871   London to Amble
        Amble to North Sunderland (manure)
        Ipswich to Amble
        Amble to Holy Island (coal)
1872   Cullen to Amble. Capt. J. Henderson.
        Amble to Hamburg (bricks)

On 30 July 1872 she was sold to James Burgon and William Craig, both Eyemouth fishermen, and transferred to Berwick registry on 24 March 1873.

The *Garibaldi* was wrecked off Aberdeen during March 1876.

53   *GEORGE* (1836-1837)

Sloop with running bowsprit   34 tons   43 x 13·6 x 7·5 feet
1828: Built Leith.
Owners. *16.5.1836:* Francis Foster (m.t.), Alnmouth.
Master. *16.5.1836:* Henry Grey.

On 8 August 1837 the *George* was sold to Thomas Aberdeen, a Newcastle master mariner. He only had her until 6 January 1838 when she was transferred to Pool, Dorset, registration.

54   *GLORIANA* (1860-1896)   O/N 28586

Snow   169 tons   94 x 23·1 x 12·9 feet
17.9.1860: Launched from Amble yard of Sanderson & Leighton.
1899: Reduced to brigantine rig.
Owners: *25.9.1860:* James Shotton (24/64), James Calder (24/64) & David Ditchburn (8/64, m.m.), all Amble; John Dryden (8/64, architect), Newcastle. *20.1.1871:* Shotton transferred his 24/64ths to Ditchburn. *30.11.1890:* David Ditchburn died. *27.4.1896:* John & James Harrison, Amble ship wrights.

At the time of her launch, the *Gloriana* was described as a: "beautiful model brig intended for the Southern Trade." However she seems to have spent most of her career trading to the Baltic in the summer and coastwise during the winter. Her maiden voyage was a near disaster. Leaving Amble with coal for Riga she soon ran into bad weather; three men were washed overboard and drowned, bulwarks were stove. On 11 October 1860 she limped into Elsinore. Heavy weather damage was again sustained during December 1862 when on passage from Danzic (Gdansk) towards Hull. She had to put into Cuxhaven leaking, with loss of boats and cargo partly damaged.

At five in the morning of 23 January 1868, when bound from Dieppe to the Tyne, she collided off Filey with the South Shields brig *John & Isabella* loosing her bowsprit, cutwater and figurehead. Four of her crew jumped aboard the *John & Isabella*. Before the year was out the *Gloriana* was again in trouble when she struck Pan Bush Rocks, near Hauxley, on 12 December. Re-floated, a steamer towed her into Amble. Here are some of the *Gloriana's* wanderings made mainly under the command of David Ditchburn:

1870   London to Amble
        Amble to Boulonge
1872   Honfleur to Amble (Capt. Porter)
        Wisbeach to Amble
        Amble to Lubeck
1876   Cronstadt to Amble (deals and battens)
        Amble to Gothenberg
1878   Nyhamn (Ala) to Amble (timber)
1878   Amble to Cronstadt

Late in 1878 the *Gloriana* began making regular runs to Calais which continued into the 1880's.

At six-thirty on the morning of 23 April 1886 she ran onto Grain Edge, Sheerness, and remained there for nearly six hours before floating off.

On 1 June 1896 the *Gloriana* was sold to John Elliott, a South Shields shipowner. Following his death she became the property of Thomas Graden, a Newcastle provision merchant, on 30 June 1899. Three months later Graden transferred 16/64ths to Mary Elizabeth Elliott and John Reay Elliott, both of South Shields. On 7 May 1904 she was sold to Thomas James Ferguson of Limerick. He was the first of a series of owners from places outside the North-East:

> *14.3.1907:* Gloriana Sailing Ship Company, Dublin.
>
> *22.9.1910:* John Henry Davis & Charles Willcocks, Plymouth.
>
> *3.11.1910:* The Denarty & Cadeby Main Collieries Limited, London.

During 1912 she was stripped down to a hulk for service at Plymouth. Her lower masts were left to serve as derrick posts. The *Gloriana's* register was closed on 12 August 1913 when sold for breaking up at Brightlingsea.

---

55   *GRACE DARLING* (? - 1874)

Barque   381 tons   126 x 29·6 x 15·1 feet

1864: Built Summerside, Prince Edward Island, by Cresswell.

P/R: Liverpool (1864/436).

Owners. *1864:* E. Read, Prince Edward Island. *10.7.1865:* John Martin & James Flett Robb, both North Shields shipowners. *1.1868:* Re-registered at Leith. *Circa 1874* (Re-registered at North Shields. Part of her Custom House Register, giving dates and other information, is missing): Robert Richardson (48/16), Amble, & Isabella Richardson (16/64).

When North Shields owned, the *Grace Darling* made a 142 day passage from London to Algoa Bay (Port Elizabeth) in 1868. She was carrying 150 tons of coal and 178 Angora rams and ewes. Many animals died during the long passage.

On 27 February 1874, as an Amble vessel, the coke laden *Grace Darling* (Capt. Ralph Davison) ran ashore north of Rattray Head, near Peterhead, with the loss of fourteen of her fifteen man crew. She had been sighted driving past Stonehaven flying distress signals. The Stonehaven lifeboat was launched to assist but, because of the severity of the weather, could not get close. It attempted to make Aberdeen harbour but capsized on the way in. Four of the lifeboat men were washed out and drowned, afterwards the boat rightened itself. In the meantime a cable had been sent from Stonehaven to Aberdeen, warning of the approach of the distressed ships, but nothing was in readiness when the dual tragedy occurred.

Walter Runciman states, in his *Collier Brigs and their Sailors*, that: "The whole crew could have been saved by the Arbroath Lifeboat, but Davison refused to leave". A subsequent Board of Trade Inquiry into the loss of the *Grace Darling* brought out the finding that her "...loss was caused by mismanagement, the crew being served liberally with grog" - a finding much criticised by North Country seamen.

---

56   *GREEN OLIVE* (1865-1880)   O/N 49762

Snow   240 tons   101·5 x 26·25 x 14·8 feet

1865: Built Hylton, Sunderland, by Grey & Young.

Owners. *18.3.1865:* Robert Richardson (22/64, s.o.), William Edward Melrose (21/64, s.o.) & William Duncan (21/64, surgeon), all Amble. *23.12.1869:* Richardson transferred 3/64ths to George Pringle (m.m.), Amble. *23.5.1878:* Melrose died; his 21/64ths were transferred to his widow Isabella.

On 9 November 1874, when bound from the Tyne to Lisbon with coal, the *Green Olive* struck the Middle Cross Sand, off Winterton, Norfolk. After jettisoning about 50 tons of cargo she was re-floated and got into Yarmouth. In December 1875 she arrived at Amble after a passage from Cowes under the command R. Lewis. A couple of years later she went from Amble to Travemunde.

The *Green Olive's* British registration was closed on 27 June 1880 following her sale to foreign owners who appear to have been Danish. For while she bore the name *Glad* before returning to the Red Ensign under her old name in 1886 after being bought by J. Robinson of Littlehampton.

On 23 February 1897 she was wrecked on the Long Sand, near Harwich, when on passage from Sunderland towards Shoreham.

57   **HALICORE** (1859-1864)   O/N 16147
Snow   259 tons   97 x 23·2 x 15·4 feet
1853: Built Blyth by Margaret Stoveld.
Owners: *29.10.1853:* William Milburn (48/64, s.o.), Blyth, & John Turnbull (16/64, m.m.), Amble. *1.3.1859 share distribution:* William Milburn (32/64), Blyth; John Turnbull (28/64) & Thomas Turnbull (4/64, s.o.), both Amble.
Master. *29.10.1853:* John Turnbull.

The *Halicore* was probably managed from Blyth by William Milburn and may well have been considered a Blyth ship. However John Turnbull of Amble commanded her for most of her career and was a substantial shareholder.

During 1858 she made a voyage to the Kuria Muria Islands, off the Coast of what is now Muscat & Oman, for a cargo of guano. To reach there Capt. Turnbull would have had to take her around the Cape of Good Hope. A long voyage for such a small ship, but quite common in those days. He was still in command in 1864 when she made a slow 41 day from Memel (Klaipeda) to the Tyne (arrived 10 May) with a cargo of rags.

On 6 December 1864, when on passage from the Tyne to Copenhagen, the *Halicore* (Capt. Walker) was abandoned in the North Sea. She had struck a rock near New Hellesund (?), floated off then foundered.

58   **HALICORE** (1865-1868)   O/N 51381
Brig   256 tons   104·6 x 25·7 x 15·7 feet
1865: Built Southwick, Sunderland, by D.A. Douglas.
Owners. *4.1.1866:* John Turnbull (32/64, m.m.), Thomas Turnbull (6/64, s.o.) & Isaac Crane Mann (6/64, s.o.), all Amble; William Milburn (20/64, s.br.), Newcastle.

The *Halicore* (Capt. Henry Wilkinson) was on passage from Blyth to Sagua la Grande, Cuba, with a cargo of coal when at ten-thirty on the night of 5 March 1868 she went ashore in Morant Bay, Jamaica, during a heavy north-east by north gale. A report of her loss was published in the *Nassau Guardian*:

"...the captain and crew barely managed to save themselves in a small boat, and after being tossed about on the waves for ten days, without anything to eat and drink, they were picked up by the American brig *James Baker,* of Philadelphia, Captain Head, who, although short of provisions himself, gave them a share and treated them very hospitably. Capt. Head made an attempt to land Captain Wilkinson and his crew at Havana, but owing to boisterous weather and head winds, could not make that port. He succeeded, however, in landing them at Gun Cay (Bahamas, 25°34' N., 79°19' W.) on the 27th ult. (*27.3.1868*). where they received every attention possible from the lighthouse keeper, Mr. H.C. Sanders. They arrived at this port (Nassau) in the, schooner *Brothers No.2* on Monday. Capt. Wilkinson informed us that the unfortun-

51

ate man (Jas. Murray) was drowned by the capsizing of the jolly boat, and that he and the rest of the crew barely escaped with their lives, as the vessel went to pieces immediately after striking. They had no covering but the clothes they stood in to shelter them from the sun and inclemency of the weather, and the boat being very small would have been swamped if they had not continually kept bailing her out. When almost famished, a large loggerhead turtle swam around the boat several times, which was easily captured and eaten raw with avidity, the blood serving to allay their insatiable thirst. But for this interposition of Providence they would have died of starvation all that had kept life and soul together previously being seaweed and the minute crustaceans clinging to it. At one time they were in such a state of dejection that they thought of terminating their sufferings by jumping overboard, but the turtle and the sight of the brig which picked them up about an hour after its capture, diverted their minds and gave them hope. Capt. Wilkinson desires through our columns to thank Capt. Head, Mr Sanders and Captain Thomas Webster (of the *Brothers*) for their great kindness and attention in this trying emergency. Henry Luff (cook and steward), was taken to the New Providence Asylum where he lies in a precarious state. The rest of the crew are are doing well."

Despite being predominantly owned by Amble people, the *Halicore* was described by the *Nassau Guardian* as a Newcastle ship which would indicate that William Milburn (owner of 20/64ths) of Newcastle was managing owner. Previously recorded as being resident in Blyth (See *Halicore*, Fleet No. 57) he had an office in Newcastle from where the ships he had an interest in were managed. Milburn later went on to be a very prosperous ship owner with a fleet of beautiful clipper-bowed steamers in the Australian trade. His firm amalgamated with others in 1914 to form what became known as the Port Line - a company well known to a more recent generation of North-East Coast seamen.

59   *HANNAH* (?1826-1846)   O/N 15420
Sloop with running bowsprit   47 tons   45·7 x 15·1 x 7·7 feet
1823: Built Dundee.
Owners. *28.2.1826:* John Skelly (32/64, farmer), Denwick, & Richard Robson (32/64, farmer), both Alnwick.
Masters. *30.6.1826:* David Moone. *3.3.1828:* George Brown. *6.3.1829:* Alexander Audison. *24.11.1829:* Richard Walker. *11.2.1840:* George Sirvan. *17.4.1844:* David Moone.

Following the death of John Skelly the *Hannah* was transferred to David Moone, of North Sunderland, on 30 June 1846. Probably the same David Moone who had been master of her on a couple of occasions. On 11 August 1862 Ann Robinson, a spinster of Holy Island, acquired 32/64ths. The *Hannah* was again sold on 2 May 1867 to John & Thomas Armstrong (32/64ths each, both carpenters) of Newcastle.

Her new owners only had her for seven months before she was wrecked near Berwick with the loss of all hands. Preserved with the *Hannah's* register in Tyne & Wear Archives is the following letter, dated 18 December 1867, written by John Armstrong to the Collector of Customs at Newcastle:

"I John Armstrong, managing owner of the sloop "Hannah" belonging to the Port of Newcastle do Hereby certify that the above named vessel was lost near Berwick on Tweed on the 2nd day of December 1867 and all hands on board the said vessel were drowned namely William Calvert, master, & John Craig, mate, and no papers belonging to the said vessel have been saved."

60   **HANNAH PARK** (1865)   O/N 7395
Snow   260 tons   98·1 x 25·3 x 16·1 feet
1856: Built Sunderland by W. Crown.
Owners. *22.7.1856:* Duncan McBrayne (s.o.), Sunderland. *10.3.1865:* John Turnbull (32/64, s.o.) & Thomas Turnbull (8/64, s.o.), both Amble; Isaac Crane Mann (8/64, m.m.), Warkworth; William Milburn (16/64, s.o.), Newcastle.

On 14 September 1865 the *Hannah Park* was run down and sunk in the Baltic by the iron steamer *Lena* of London.

61   **HARE BELL** (1879-1890)   O/N 49630
Brig   249 tons   102 ·6 x 26 x 14·6 feet
1864: Built Newcastle by Hutchinson.
Owners. *20.9.1864:* George Cunningham Hutchinson (s.b.), Newcastle. *24.11.1864:* William Miekle (rope manufacturer), Newcastle acquired 8/64ths. *26.1.1865:* Hutchinson transferred 16/64ths to David Moffat (draper), Newcastle. *23.12.1867:* Hutchinson transferred 4/64ths to William Prior (m.m.), Blyth. *20.5.1870 share distribution:* David Moffat (16/64), Newcastle; William Prior (4/64), Blyth; John Henry Gibb (21/64, m.m.), Amble; William Milburn (23/64, s.br.), Newcastle. *17.11.1879 share distribution:* John Henry Gibb (19/64, m.m.), Thomas Leighton (4/64, grocer), John Glass (5/64, school master), John Park (7/64, clerk), Michael Wilson (5/64, engineer), Martin Forrest Gray (6/64, harbour master), William Gair (4/64, m.m.) and Thomas Lamb (5/64, innkeeper), all Amble; Andrew Scott (5/64, colliery manager), Broomhill; William Prior (4/64), Blyth.

Before becoming an Amble ship, the *Hare Bell* made a number of voyages in the South American trades making a passage from the Tyne to Rio de Janeiro in 1864. On 29 January 1868 when bound from Santa Marta, Columbia, to Bremen with a valuable cargo of tobacco, coffee, cotton, nuts and ivory she ran ashore near Pigeon Island in the West Indies. A warship was sent to her assistance and she was got off.

Here are some passages, made under the command of John H. Gibb, when first Amble owned:

1879	Windau (Ventspils) to London
	(arrived 12 August)
1880/81	Malaga to Elsinore 29 days.
	Elsinore (sailed 23.8.1880) to Stettin (Szczecin)
	Mandel to Grimsby (arrived 22 January)
1882	Amble (sailed 17 January) to Lisbon
	(Capt. John H. Gibb)
	Lisbon to Vlaardingen (arrived 14 April)
1883	Amble (10 March) to Boulogne

In July 1890 the *Hare Bell* was acquired by Bessy & Palmer of Yarmouth but continued to make visits to the North-East Coast for coal cargoes. During March 1898, when bound from Yarmouth towards Sunderland in ballast, she went ashore near North Somercoates; was re-floated only to go ashore again eight months later at Gorleston.

In about 1920 she became the property of John W. Robertson of Lerwick. Her name lingered on in *Lloyd's Register* well into the 1930's.

62   **HARMONY** (1854-1855)
Schooner   56 tons   54 x 15·4 x 8·9 feet
1841: Built Garmouth.
P/R: Banff (1849/26)

Owners. *4.10.1854:* Sold by James Richie & Lewis Chalmers, Aberdeen, to James Sanderson (32/64, s.b.) & Thomas Leighton (32/64, s.o.), both Amble.
Master. *22.11.1854:* Thomas Anderson.

On 20 January 1855 the *Harmony* was transferred to William Rugg (33/64, carpenter), of Lyme, and Edward Miller (31/64, mariner), Beer, Devon. she was transferred to the Lyme Register a couple of weeks later.

63   *HARRIET* (1855-?)   O/N 7638
Barque   275 tons   106·5 x 26· x 15·9 feet
1855: Built Sunderland by P. Forrest.
Owners. *29.11.1855:* Henry Henderson (22/64) & Thomas Henderson (21/64), both Warkworth shipowners; Jane Elizabeth Henderson (21/64, spinster), North Shields.

At an undetermined date the *Harriet* was sold to foreigners.

64   *HAYS* (1867-1871)   O/N 56517
Brig   294 tons   106 x 26·5 x 16·8 feet
1867: Built Seaham by Potts.
Owners. *22.10.1867:* William Charles Hay, Amble.

On 5 January 1871 the *Hays* was sold to Isaac Bedlington of West Hartlepool, and Henry Taylor, Sunderland.

She was wrecked near Belfast on 20 December 1872.

65   *HELEN RICHARDS* (1862-1879)   O/N 44302
Brig   184 tons   95·7 x 24·7 x 13·3 feet
1862: Built Hylton, Sunderland, by Todd.
Owners. *19.7.1862:* John Henderson (34/64, plumber) & John Darling (8/64, m.m.), both Amble, and William Thompson (22/64, plumber), Blyth. *5.4.1866:* Thompson transferred his 22/64ths to Henderson. *5.3.1867:* John Henderson became sole owner. *1.7.1875:* John Henderson died.

During December 1867, when bound from Ancona to Plymouth with wheat, the *Helen Richards* (Capt. Hogg) put into Tunis in a damaged condition. On what was probably her last voyage as an Amble ship she went to the Baltic, under the command of Capt. Waringer, calling at Reval (Tallinn) on 31 May 1879. In the following September Benjamin James, a Sunderland ship master, acquired her. Three months later, on Christmas Day, she struck the wreck of a Glasgow steamer near the Haisborough Sand. Lucky to be got off she was towed into Lowestoft by the tug *Comet*. More trouble occurred on 15 July 1880 when entering Ramsgate Harbour. Laden with a cargo of coal, she struck the West Pier and carried away bowsprit and jib-boom.

On 21 October 1882 the *Helen Richards* left Sunderland for Littlehampton and was never seen again. Benjamin James was in command; his son was aboard with him.

66   *HENRY* (1864-1865)   O/N 43503
Fore and aft schooner   46 tons   65·7 x 15·7 x 6·8 feet
1849: Built Port Downie, Sterling.
P/R: Leith (1861/19).
Owners. *25.2.1864:* William Gray (fish merchant), Amble.

On 20 November 1865 the *Henry* foundered in the Fidra Roads, at the southern entrance of the Firth of Forth, when on passage from Bowness towards Berwick.

67   *HERMON* (1869-1888)   O/N 60510
Barque   391 tons   132·3 x 28 x 17 feet
1869: Built Sunderland by Benjamin Hodgson.
Owners. *3.3.1869:* Andrew Richardson (24/64, managing owner), Amble; William Davison (4/64), Robert Davison (12/64) & David McKenley (4/64), all Alnwick shipowners; George Marshall (2/64, s.o.), Killingworth; John Duthie (18/64, s.o.), Cairnbulg, Aberdeen. *5.3.1869:* Richardson transferred 2/64ths to Thomas Smith Howitt, a Warkworth shipowner. *12.11.1874:* Andrew Richardson transferred 8/64ths to William Richardson (medical student) and 2/64ths to John Marshall Duncan Turner (draper), both Amble. *30.3.1887:* Andrew Richardson died. *4.12.1887:* Thomas Smith Howitt, Warkworth, acquired shares (22/64ths) of Andrew & William Richardson.

On 19 January 1888 the *Hermon* (Capt. Duthie) was wrecked on Half Moon Cay Reef (17°12' N., 87°33' W.), off the Coast of Honduras.

68   *HIAWATHA* (1883-1888)   O/N 65530
Brig   280 tons   116·1 x 26·5 x 14.9 feet
1871: Built Enmore River, Prince Edward Island, by George Bollum.
P/R: Swansea (1872/18).
Owners. *30.1.1883:* Hugh Andrews (coal owner), Felton, managed by John Park, Warkworth Harbour. *11.4.1888:* Henry Edward Pyle Adamson (s.o.), Newcastle.

As an Amble ship the *Hiawatha* carried coal from her home port to Chatham, Calais, Copenhagen, and Christiania (Oslo), as well as many other destinations, all under the command of Capt. Jackson. In 1885 she went from Amble to Barbados in 43 days arriving on 23 December. From Barbados she was ordered to Trinidad to discharge her coal before going to Mobile to load logs for Amble.

On 11 April 1888 the *Hiawatha* was sold to Henry Edward Pyle Adamson, a Newcastle shipowner. He had her until 2 August when sold to William Wright, a merchant of Sulina, Roumania. A month later her Custom House Register was closed and endorsed: "dismantled and converted to a lighter".

69   *HOPE* (1852-1853)
Brig   130 tons   71·8 x 20·9 x 12·8 feet
1817: Built Sculcoates, York.
Owners. *27.7.1852:* Sold by William Weatherill, Whitby, to Thomas & Henry Henderson (16/64ths each), Warkworth merchants; John James Henderson (16/64, m.t.) & Jane Elizabeth Henderson (16/64, spinster), both North Shields.
Master. *3.8.1852:* James Dennison.

On 22/23 January 1853 the *Hope* was wrecked on rocks near Redcar.

70   *HOTSPUR* (1826-1846)
Sloop with running bowsprit   55 tons   47·4 x 14·4 x 8·2 feet
1826: Built Dundee.
Owners. *18.4.1826:* John Skelly (32/64, farmer), Denwick, & Richard Robson (32/64, farmer), Alnwick.
Masters. *14.2.1827:* William Walker. *26.11.1842:* George Swan. *11.1.1844:* James Morn.

Following the death of John Skelly the *Hotspur* was acquired by Alexander Emery, a Beadnell merchant, on 6 May 1846. He had her until 27 December 1853 when James Sinclair, a Berwick commission agent, became owner. She was transferred to Leith registration on 5 June 1854.

71   *HUMILITY* (?1825-1833)
Schooner   76 tons   60 x 17 feet
1817: Built Hull.
P/R: Berwick (1822/3)
Owners. *17.10.1825:* Edward Gibb (16/64, m.m.) & Thomas Simpson (16/64, victualler), both Alnmouth.
Master. *17.10.1825:* Matthew Simpson.
On 23 Septemberr 1833 the *Humility* was sold to George Ritchie, Pulteney Town, Wick, and transferred to that port.

72   *HUMILITY* (1851-1862)   O/N 2442
Snow   205 tons   86·4 x 21·7 x 13·9 feet
1851: Built Blyth by Bowman & Drummond.
Owners. *22.3.1851:* Robert Simpson (32/64), Edward Thomas Simpson (8/32) & George Potter (12/64), all Alnmouth; James Heatley (12/64, m.m.), Blyth.
Master: *22.3.1851:* James Heatley.
On 15 May 1862 the *Humility* (Capt. Davis) capsized off Eartholms, Bornholm Island, when on passage from Danzic towards London. She was later found by a steamer two miles east of the island "bottom up". Three days later her wreck was sold for breaking up. No lives were lost.

73   *HUMILITY* (1862-1863)   O/N 44301
Snow   250 tons   98·7 x 36 x 15·4 feet
1862: Built South Hylton, Sunderland.
Owners. *15.7.1862:* James Heatley (20/64, agent), Amble; George Potter (20/64, s.o.), Robert Simpson (20/64, s.o.) & Matthew George Simpson (4/64, agent), all Alnmouth.
The *Humility* was abandoned in the North Sea during a severe gale on 21 December 1863. Her register was not closed until 10 March 1887!

74   *HUNTLEYS* (1865-1879)   O/N 49789
Snow   186 tons   92·x 24·1 x 13·4 feet
2.10.1865: Launched at Pallion, Sunderland, from yard of James Robinson.
1883: Reduced to brigantine rig.
Owners. *12.10.1865:* John Turner (28/64, s.o.), William Edward Melrose (8/64, s.o.), Robert Matthews (8/64, pilot) & John Robert Jackson (8/64, m.m.), all Amble. *23.5.1878:* William Edward Melrose died.
At her launch it was noted that the *Huntleys* was intended for the Baltic trade and had Cunningham's patent reefing topsails fitted. In 1868, during the course of a passage from Cronstadt towards Waterford, she took 24 days to reach the North Foreland. Later in the same year she arrived in the Yarmouth Roads, leaky, when on passage from Middlesborough to Dunkirk. Here are some of her later passages, all made under the command of Capt. Jackson:

                    1872   Amble to St Petersburg
                    1874   Amble to Copenhagen
                    1876   Cronstadt to Amble
                            Amble to Elsinore
                    1878   Amble to Lisbon

On 28 August 1879 she was sold to George Herbert Gann, a shipowner of Whitstable, Kent. Six days later he transferred 32/64ths to Henry Gann of the same place. The *Huntleys* was transferred to Faversham in November 1885. In 1912 she is listed as being owned by the

Whitstable Shipping Company of Whitstable, Kent.

During 1916, J.K. Morris of Liverpool became owner. He did not have her for long. On 25 March 1917, when on passage from Bristol towards Dieppe with a cargo of pitch, she was captured by a German submarine 28 miles S.S.W of Beachy Head and destroyed by explosives - a fate shared by many sailing ships during the First World War.

75   **INCONSTANT** (1878-1884)   O/N 2425
Brigantine   161 tons   87·4 x 19·7 x 13·5 feet
1839: Built Aberdeen.
P/R: Aberdeen (1843/33)
Owners. *7.9.1849:* James Turnbull (25/64), Blyth; George Dobson (or Gibson)(21/64) & William Winship (18/64), both Cowpen. *23.1.1874:* James Turnbull (32/64); James Turnbull & John Robert Foster (jointly 32/64), all Blyth. *8.4.1878:* James Turnbull (32/64) & James Turnbull jun. (32/64), both Blyth. *9.7.1878:* Hugh Andrews, Felton Park, & 25, Queen Street, Newcastle. *17.12.1878:* John Park, Warkworth, appointed manager.

When she first became an Amble ship the *Inconstant* made a couple of coal laden voyages to Trouville under the command of Capt. Poole. On 21 October 1878 she sustained serious damage following a collision with the steamer *Agnes & Louisa*. Capt. Poole was still in command when she was run down and sunk in the Corton Roads, off Great Yarmouth, on 2 February 1884.

76   **ISABELLA & MARY** (1856-1869)
Snow   181 tons   92·9 x 22·2 x 13·3 feet
4.6.1856: Launched at Amble from yard of Sanderson & Leighton.
Owners. *4.7.1856:* Jeffrey Heatley (8/64, draper), Henry Heatley (24/64, s.o.), Robert Gibb (16/64) & John Henry Gibb (16/64), Alnmouth.

Intended for the southern trade, the *Isabella & Mary* was built of oak from Whitehouse Wood, near Alnwick. Her first master was John Henry Gibb. On 12 January 1869 she was lost in the Thames.

77   **ISABELLA WATT** (?1825-1829)
Schooner   75 tons   54 x 18 feet
1814: Built Elie.
P/R: Berwick (1823/1)
Owners. *25.10.1825:* John Wilkinson (m.t.), High Buston.
Master. *25.10.1825:* Daniel Whiteman.

The *Isabella Watt* was lost on 8 April 1829.

78   **ISABELLAS** (1856-1874)(1875-1876)   O/N 2452
Snow   133 tons   84 x 22·1 x 12·2 feet
1856: Built Blyth by Bowman & Drummond.
1873: Re-rigged as brigantine.
Owners. *25.2.1856:* James Allen (32/64, draper), Alnwick; Robert Hedley (24/64, m.m.) & Thomas Young (4/64, inn keeper), both Amble; Thomas Hedley Willis (4/64, miller), Lesbury. *11.10.1856:* Hedley transferred 4/64ths jointly to Joseph Foley & Alexander Aikonow, London ship brokers. *20.2.1864:* James Allen (32/64), Robert Hedley (12/64), Thomas Young (16/64) & Thomas Hedley Willis (4/64).

In the early 1870's the *Isabellas* traded regularly to Boulogne under the command of N. Mather and T. Young. On 11 November 1874 her register was closed when sold to foiegners. Just over twelve months later, on 28 December 1875, she came back under the

Red Ensign when Thomas Young of Amble, one of her previous share holders, bought her. She remained under his ownership until 16 August 1876 when Alfred Charles Perkins, a Whitstable shipwright, became owner. A week later he transferred 22/64ths to George Herbert Gann and 21/64ths to Henry Gann, both Whitstable shipowners.

The *Isabellas* register was cancelled on 28 February 1905 after she had been wrecked near Lowestoft.

79   *JANE* (1849-1850)   O/N 9049
Snow   136 tons   74·7 x 18·8 x 11·5 feet
1823: Built Elie, Fife.
P/R: Aberdeen (1839/28).
1847: Enlarged at Newcastle by William Rennison to above dimensions.
Owners. *28.1.1847:* Thomas Hood Henderson, Newcastle, sold her to Edward Whitfield (m.t.), Newcastle. *1.1.1848:* Whitfield transferred 16/64ths to Henry Heatley (m.m.), Alnmouth. *17.8.1849:* Heatley became sole owner.
Masters. *24.7.1847:* William Starling. *4.3.1848:* Henry Heatley.

On 26 November 1849, while attempting to enter Amble Harbour with a heavy sea from the south-east, the *Jane* was driven ashore on the end of the North Pier and was badly damaged. At the following flood tide she surged off and sunk in the entrance of the Coquet. She was re-floated and transferred to Berwick registration on 8 March 1850.

At 3 p.m., on the afternoon of 22 January 1860, when on passage from Amble to Boulogne, the *Jane* (Capt. Andrew Heatley) sprung a leak and foundered about forty miles off Flamborough Head. Her crew were saved.

80   *JANE & ELEANOR* (1862-1873)   O/N 44292
Brig   197 tons   96·2 x 24·2 x 13·5 feet
1862: Built Sunderland by B.& J. Gardner.
Owners. *12.5.1862:* John Henry Barry (20/64, s.o.), Jane Douglas (20/64, widow) & John Fernhill Holdsworth (8/64, farmer), all Amble; Jane Hudson (8/64, widow) & Margaret Hudson (8/64, spinster), both Felton. *3.3.1870:* Jane Douglas died; her 20/64ths transferred to Barry. *8.12.1870:* Holdsworth transferred his 8/64ths to Barry.

The *Jane & Eleanor* went missing after leaving Falmouth on 30 January 1873.

81   *JANE BROWN* (1865-1888)   O/N 49755
Brig   298 tons   107·8 x 26·7 x 16·5 feet
1865: Built North Hylton, Sunderland, by Gibbon & Nichol.
Owners. *16.1.1865:* Andrew Richardson (26/64) & Thomas Richardson (16/64), both Amble shipowners; Luke Richardson (8/64, s.o.), Willington; John Duthie (14/64, s.o.), Cairnbulg, Aberdeen. *21.2.1868:* Andrew Richardson transferred 8/64ths to Thomas Brown, (m.t.), Warkworth. *2.7.1868:* Andrew Richardson transferred his remaining 18/64ths to William Richardson (medical student), Amble. *17.8.1876:* Andrew Richardson, Reading, became managing owner. *17.5.1886:* Thomas Richardson died. *17.2.1888:* Richards 16/64ths transferred jointly to George Duncan, Newcastle, & John Wesley Richards, Alnwick. *25.7.1888 share distribution:* Luke Richardson (8/64), John Duthie (14/64), Thomas Smith Howitt(34/64, s.o.), Reading, & Mary Brown (8/64, widow), Forrest Hall, Newcastle.

The *Jane Brown's* register was closed on 11 August 1888 after her sale to A. Pederson of Sandvigen, near Arendal, Norway. However a couple of years later she returned to British ownership when acquired by W.B.S. Anholm of Aberdeen.

On 7 January 1891 the *Jane Brown* was wrecked near San Domingo (Ciudad Trujillo), Dominica, when on passage to Liverpool.

82   *JOHN* (1835-1838)

Sloop (originally a keel)   69 tons   51 x 18 x 6·7 feet
1793: Built at Stella, near Blaydon-on-Tyne, by John Tate.
1835: Re-built & altered to sloop rig at Blyth by Bowman & Drummond.
Owner. *15.1.1835:* George Fawcus (farmer), Dunston Square.
Master. *15.1.1835:* Thomas Fawcus.

On 3 May 1838 the *John* was transferred to Newcastle when acquired by John Ingo (22/64, s.o.), Thomas Jameson (21/64, m.m.) & Robert Cummings (21/64, butcher) of that port. In turn she became the property of:

3.1.1840: John Adams (s.b.), North Shore, Newcastle.
12.9.1840: Thomas Jamieson re-acquired 32/64ths.
21.4.1841: John Adams transferred his 32/64ths to Lancelot Adams (glass manufacturer), Hartley.
16.11.1841: Lancelot Adams transferred his 32/64ths to Robert Gilray, (engineer), Tynemouth.
4.5.1843: Gilray transferred his 32/64ths to James Hedley (m.t.), Newcastle.
10.6.1843: George Little (22/64, m.t.), Monkwearmouth; William Cooper (21/64), High Felling, & Richard Dalton (21/64), Gateshead.

On 20 November 1851, the *John* (Capt. John Straughan) was lost at Northoar (? North Gare) on the River Tees.

83   *JOHN ELLISON* (1845-1848)

Brig   216 tons   84·5 x 22·7 x 14·1 feet
1845: Built Southwick, Sunderland, by Doxford & Crown.
Owners. *12.6.1845:* Thomas Browne, Amble. *18.6.1845:* Thomas Douglas (m.m.), Sunderland, acquired 2/64ths. *31.12.1846:* Browne again became sole owner.
Master. *12.6.1845:* Thomas Douglas.

On 27 November 1848 the *John Ellison* was transferred to Faversham, and lost a year or two later.

84   *JOHN WHITE* (1837-1848)

Snow   210 tons   88 x 24·7 x 15 feet
1831: Built Sunderland by John Brunton.
Owners. *3.3.1831:* Andrew & Richard White (21/64 each), John White (22/64), all Bishopwearmouth shipowners. *30.12.1835:* William Thompson (baker), Monkwearmouth. *1.3.1837:* William & Luke Hindmarch, Alnwick merchants.

On 25 April 1848 the *John White* was sold to Robert Jolly, a South Shields merchant. She foundered off Whitby on 27 December 1852.

85   *KEDRON* (1866-1885)   O/N 56473

Barque   373 tons   121·5 x 27·8 x 17·3 feet
1866: Built Hylton, Sunderland, by B. Hodgson.
Owners. *22.11.1866:* Andrew Richardson (22/64, s.o.), Thomas Richardson (8/64, s.o.) & John Marshall Duncan Turner (4/64, draper), all Amble; Thomas Brown (8/64, builder) George Horritt (11/64, cordwainer), both Warkworth; Luke Richardson (8/64, s.o.), Willington Quay; William Marshall (3/64, agriculturalist), Lesbury. *8.2.1868:* George Horritt transf-

erred 2/64ths each to Adam & Robert Horritt (cordwainers) and Thomas Smith Horritt (m.m.), all Warkworth. *6.6.1868:* Andrew Richardson transferred 4/64ths to William Richardson (medical student), Amble, 3/64ths to Margaret Duncan (spinster), Alnwick, and 1/64th to George Marshall (labourer), North Shields.

On 20 September 1884 the *Kedron* was reported to have left Mauritius for Bombay. In the following year, on 9 December, when on passage from Cochin towards Riga with "dying wood", she went ashore at Domesness (Kolka), Latvia. After going aground her master, Capt. Clark, went ashore in one of the boats to telegraph Riga for a tug and lighter. During the night a north-west gale sprang up. At day break, when the tug arrived, the *Kedron* was lying on her side with only the tops of her masts visible. The bodies of Capt. Clark and the first mate were later washed ashore. Capt. Clark, of Vicarage Street, North Shields, had been sent to Spain to take command of the *Kedron* only a few weeks before. He was to bring her to Domesness following the death of her previous master who was his brother-in-law.

86   *KENTISH TAR* (1877-1887)
Barque   570 net 590 gross tons   152 x 30·7 x 18 feet (L/R)
1877: Built Sunderland by R. Thompson.
Registered in London.
Owners. *1877 L/R:* G. Simpson & Co., Paikes Street, Alnwick. *1885 Turnbull's Register:* G. Simpson (12/64) & D. McKenley (28/64), both Alnwick; A. Thompson (4/64), Sunderland; W. Wood (20/64), Faversham, Kent.
During 1882 the *Kentish Tar* (Capt. Veitch) went from Batavia (Djakarta) to Padang where she arrived on 9 March to load for New York.
In 1887 she was re-named *G.N. Wilcox* when acquired by J.G.C. Henoch (J.C. Pflinger, manager), of Bremen. Two years later A. Burchard of Rostock became owner. On 13 October 1893 she was wrecked at Grande Point (25°7' S., 70°34'2 W.), Peru, when on a Cape Horn passage from Hamburg towards Antofagasta.

87   *KESTREL* (1853-1855)   O/N 25639
Barque   325 tons   97 x 23·9 x 16·9 feet
24.10.1839: Launched at North Shields by T.& W. Smith.
Owners. *4.1.1840*: Thomas & William Smith (jointly 48/64), and Thomas Smith (m.t.), Newcastle, & William Alderson Reed (m.m.), Walker (jointly 16/64). *1853:* William Alderson Reed died. *16.12.1853:* Luke Hindmarsh, Alnwick.
Master: *21.12.1853:* John Lindsay.
The *Kestrel* was built for the East India trade. On her maiden voyage as a Tyne owned ship she was advertised to sail for "the Cape of Good Hope". On 16 February 1849 she arrived at Singapore after being "plundered by a pirate brigantine of about 200 tons and a crew of about fifty hands".
Her Alnwick owner put the *Kestrel* into the more prosaic Baltic trade. On her final voyage she left Liverpool for Memel (Klaipeda) but on 24 August 1855 foundered after striking a uncharted rock near the Island of Canna, off the West Coast of Scotland. Her crew were saved.

88   *KING JOHN* (1868-1872)   O/N 25596
Barque   301 tons   109·3 x 26·4 x 17 feet
1854: Built Sunderland by Ratcliffe & Spence.
P/R: Lynn (1857/4)
Owner. *29.10.1868:* John Marshall (s.o.), Amble.
On 5 November 1872 the *King John* was wrecked on Eckless Island, Gulf of Bothnia.

89   **KISHON** (1872-1890)
Barque   473 tons   143 x 29·3 x 18 feet
1872: Built Sunderland by James Gardner.
Owners. *14.10.1872:* Andrew Richardson (32/64, s.o.) & Thomas Smith Howitt (32/64, m.m.), both Amble. *28.11.1872:* Andrew Richardson transferred 4/64ths each to Thomas Richards (s.o.), Blyth, & Thomas Brown (s.o.), Newcastle, and 3/64ths to George Marshall (clerk), Newcastle. *29.6.1877:* Andrew Richardson transferred a further 3/64ths to Matthew Dixon and 1/64th jointly to Clarinda Lydia Gatley & Louisa Caroline Gatley (spinsters), St Marys, Cornwall. *17.5.1886:* Thomas Richards died. *1.3.1888 share distribution*: Thomas Smith Howitt (53/64), George Marshall (3/64), Thomas Brown (4/64), Matthew Dixon (3/64) & the Misses Gatley (jointly 1/64).

At the end of a passage from Algoa Bay (Port Elizabeth) to London, under the command of Thomas Smith Howitt, the *Kishon* was being towed to Appledore by the tug *Australia* for refitting when, on 7 November 1890, the tow rope parted. She went ashore near Bude, Cornwall. Her crew was rescued by the local Rocket Brigade.

90   **LADY MATHESON** (1866-1877)   O/N 20733
Brigantine   150 tons   81·9 x 23·3 x 12·2 feet
1849: Built Barth, Prussia.
P/R: Stornoway (1857/1).
Owners. *2.7.1866:* Sold by Donald Mackenzie, Stornoway, to John Duncan (s.o.), Amble.

In the early 1870's the *Lady Matheson* made a number of coal laden runs to Boulogne under the command of J. Lodge. On 20 November 1877 she was sold to Benjamin James, a Yarmouth shipowner, and Mary Ann Allison, a Sunderland widow. Benjamin James was the managing owner.

She was run down and sunk off Scarborough by the West Hartlepool steamer *Jeannie* on 7 September 1879.

91   **LADY NEPEAN** (1838-1845)
Schooner   81 tons   57 x 19·1 x 9·4 feet
1803: Built Bridport, Dorset.
1839: Enlarged by Bowman & Drummond, Blyth.
New dimensions: 110 tons   67 x 17.5 x 10 feet
P/R: London (1837/348).
Owners. *8.3.1838:* William Apsen, James Smith, David Griffith & William Gibbs, Rotherhithe, to Thomas Browne, Amble House, Warkworth.
Masters: *15.3.1838:* Robert Weatherly. *6.8.1839:* Henry Heatly.

The *Lady Nepean* was the first ship to be acquired by Thomas Browne who was to become, in a short period of time, one of Amble's largest shipowners.

During May 1845, she was lost off Harwich.

92   **LANCASTER** (1852-1855)   O/N 26126
Brig   94 tons   82·9 x 19·9 x 13·8 feet
1840: Built Glasson.
Owners. *29.12.1852:* Sold by Josias Booker, Allerton, Lancaster, to James Shotton (16/64, butcher) & John Muras (13/64, m.m.), both Amble; John Shotton (16/64, shoe maker), Robert Green (13/64, agent) & Donald McInnes (6/64, grocer), all Warkworth.
Master. *24.1.1853:* John Muras.

On 29 August 1855 the *Lancaster* was sold to Thomas Tindle, a West Hartlepool master mariner. He was followed by the following Seaham Harbour owners:

17.4.1873: George Judson (m.m.).

21.4.1873: William Watson (s.o.).

She was reported to have been abandoned on 15 October 1877.

93   **LANDSCAPE** (1851-1872)   O/N 8501

Brig   185 tons   85 x 21·4 x 13·4 feet

1851: Built Amble by John Bergen.

Owners. *1.7.1851:* George, Robert & Andrew Richardson (16/64 each), all Amble; Robert Mann (16/64, m.m.), Clay, Norfolk. *5.2.1852:* Following death of Robert Mann, George & Robert Richardson acquired 4/64ths each and Thomas Richards (m.m.), Shoreham, 8/64ths of his shares.

Masters. *7.10.1850:* William Quack. *1.7.1851:* Robert Mann. *30.8.1851:* Thomas Sheet. *8.1.1852:* Thomas Richards.

In 1863, when on passage from Cronstadt to London, the *Landscape* (Capt. Dixon) passed Aldboro when 31 days out.

At two o'clock on the afternoon of 4 April 1870 she collided, off Dimlington, with the coal laden schooner *Fifeshire*, of Colchester, which went down in a shipping lane leaving only her topmasts visible above the water. The *Landscape's* (Capt. Wheatley) stem was split and decks started. She was towed into Grimsby for repairs which took three weeks. This incident was followed by a run from Amble to Copenhagen with coal.

On 12 February 1872, when on passage from Amble towards Boulogne, the *Landscape* struck Corton Sand, near Great Yarmouth, and foundered almost immediately. Her crew were rescued by the steam tug *Express* and landed at the Norfolk port.

94   **LEBANON** (1867-1879)   O/N 56484

Snow   199 tons   93·6 x 24·4 x 13·9 feet

1867: Built Sunderland by James Robinson.

Owners. *1867:* R.G. McInnes & Co., Amble.

Early in her career the *Lebanon* appears to have made a voyage from Blyth to South America. She later traded to the Baltic. Eighteen seventy-nine, her final year, was a catalogue of disasters:

May: When making a ballast passage between the Swedish ports of Helsingborg to Pas Kallavik, went ashore at Ostley, on the Island of Oland.

24 October: Stranded on the Middle Cross Sand, off Yarmouth. Re-floated and re-paired Laing's Yard, Sunderland.

Finally, on 13 November the *Lebanon* (Capt. Stevens) went ashore on the north-east side of the Island of Laeso, in the Kattegat, when on passage from Helsingborg to Bristol with oats. Her crew were saved.

95   **LILY** (1882-1889)   O/N 52095

Brigantine   235 tons   108·9 x 27· x 12·2 feet

1866: Built Kempt, Hants County, Nove Scotia, by James A. Stawatt.

Owners. *29.5.1882:* Hugh Andrews (s.o.), Eastfield Hall, Northumberland. *3.7.1882:* John Park, Warkworth Harbour, appointed manager. *2.10.1889:* John Edward Cutter (m.t.), Morpeth.

During 1880 the *Lily* made a fast, four day passage from Amble to Elsinore under the command of Capt. Jackson. In the following year a round voyage was made from Amble to Calais and back.

On 30 November 1889 she became a wreck after stranding in Galway Bay.

96 *LIZZIE BARRY* O/N 72131

Barque 498 tons 146·6 x 30·1 x 18·1 feet (L/R)

1876: Built Sunderland by J. Gardner.

Registered in Whitby.

Owners. This vessel (spelt *Lizzie Barrie*) is listed in *Amble & District* by T.L. McAndrew as belonging to J.H. Barrie of Amble but this is not born out in contemporary shipping registers. *1876 L/R:* J.H. Barry, Whitby. *1895 Turnbull's Maritime Register:* J.H. Barry (19/64), F. Richardson & W.S. Gray (jointly 8/64) & J. Robinson (8/64), all Gateshead.

During 1887 the *Lizzie Barry* became the property of Cia Esplotadora de Lota y Coronel, Chile, and was re-named *Luz*. In 1910, N. Pasaque of Callao is recorded as being owner. She lingered on in *Lloyd's Register* until being deleted in 1923, without comment. Many old British square-riggers spent their last years in the guano trade on the West Coast of South America.

97 *LUCK'S ALL* (1863-1869) O/N 45618

Schooner 26 tons 47·8 x 15·3 x 6·3 feet

1863: Built Amble.

Owner. *11.8.1863:* John Henderson (m.t.), Hauxley.

During September 1869 the *Luck's All* was broken up at Hauxley.

98 *LYRA*

Brig 197 tons

1852: Built Whitby.

Owners. Listed in *Amble & District* by T.L. McAndrews as belonging to J.H. Barrie, Amble, but this is not born out in *Lloyd's Register* which gives the following: *1856:* Barry & Co., Whitby.

The *Lyra* was not listed in *Lloyd's Register* after *1860*.

99 *MAID OF ALN* (1841-1860)

Schooner 108 tons 74·6 x 18 x 10 feet

1841: Built Aberdeen by Alexander Hall & Sons. Cost £1,400.

Owners. *7.8.1841:* Robert Simpson (16/64, wharfinger) & Henry George Gibb (16/64, m.m.), both Alnmouth; Edward Thew (32/64, m.t.), Alnwick.

Master. *7.8.1841:* Henry Gibb. *8.2.1850:* George John Stanton. *30.8.1853:* David Ditchburn.

The *Maid of Aln* was transferred to Arbroath on 31 October 1860 when acquired by A. Roy. She was then described as a collier. She was then described as a collier. At five o'clock on the morning of 21 December 1863 she struck the Goldstone Rock (two miles east-south-east of Emanuel Head, Holy Island) and went down in five minutes.

At the time of her loss, the *Maid of Aln* was on passage from Arbroath towards Sunderland under the command of John Spalding. The weather was hazy. Her five man crew had a narrow escape. The *Newcastle Daily Journal* of 22 December 1863 reported:

"The men cut the lashings of the boat and four of them got into it; the fifth was still clinging to the vessel when she sunk, but on her partially rising again he got hold of the boats stern and was drawn in. They had no oars and were driven by the flood tide to one of the Farne Islands where they were observed from another island and finally brought ashore in safety."

100   **MAID OF ALN** (1875-1886)   O/N 70397
Barque   497 tons   148 x 30·2 x 18 feet
1875: Built Hylton, Sunderland, by James Gardner.
Owners. *25.5.1875:* William Davison (17/64, s.o.,m.o.), William Dixon Spittle (4/64, m.t.), Peter Eadington (2/64, miller), Robert Thomas Grey (2/64, banker), James Horsley (4/64, m.t.), John James Horsley (4/64, m.t.), John Robert Thomas Cairns (1/64, farmer), John Davison (2/64, stationer), John Bruce (1/64, tobacconist), Henry Candlish (4/64), George Jamison Cairns (1/64, farmer), Michael Stanley Friers (4/64, tobacconist) & Robert Scott (1/64, grocer), all Alnwick; Thomas Shinn (6/64, mining engineer), Radcliffe; John Wilkinson Annett (2/64, farmer), Ulgham; Henry McQuillen (2/64) & Thomas Hutchinson (2/64, butcher), both Lesbury; William Straughan (2/64, builder), Alnmouth; John May (3/64, m.m.), Cairnbulg, Aberdeen. *18.6.1878:* George Simpson, Alnwick, appointed manager.

The *Maid of Aln* made voyages world-wide. Here are some examples:

    1880   Buenos Ayres to Rangoon.
             (Blockaded in Buenos Ayres for a long time)
    1880/81 Rangoon to London.
             (24 Jan: Passed St Helena)
    1882   Cheribon (Tjirebon) to Queenstown.
             Queenstown to Bristol (arrived 1 April)
             Cardiff (sailed 9 May) to Mauritius.
             (arrived previous to 9 August)
             Mauritius (sailed 30 Sept.) to London.

At Mauritius part of the cargo of the ship *Mars* was loaded. This vessel had put in leaky when on passage from Conconada. The *Maid of Aln's* next voyage got off to a bad start. Leaving the Tyne for Anjer, Dover was passed on 6 February 1883. Nine days later she arrived at Plymouth with cargo shifted and loss of sails.

    1884   Chittagong to Mauritus.
             Mauritus to Trinidad   90 days.
    1885   Savannah to Liverpool   30 days.

All of the above voyages were made under the command of John Smith. He was succeeded by Capt. Anderson.

    1885   Mersey to Buenos Ayres   60 days.
             Buenos Ayres to Pensacola.
             Pensacola (sailed 8 June) to Brake.

The *Maid of Aln* was abandoned at sea on 24 September 1886.

101   **MANFRED** (1871-1874)(1875-1879)   O/N 47712
Barque   586 tons   152·5 x 30·5 x 19·3 feet
1864: Built Deptford, Sunderland, by John Robinson.
Owners. *1.6.1864:* John Clay (52/64), John James Clay (8/64) & Henry T. Scott (4/64), all Sunderland. *1867:* John James Clay became bankrupt. *1.5.1871:* Luke Richardson (s.o.), Rose Hill, Northumberland. *18.5.1871:* William (12/64, s.o.), Robert (16/64, builder) & George (8/64, builder) Davison and David McKinley (16/64, builder), all Alnwick; *20.11.1874:* Sold to foreigners. *31.3.1875:* William Davison (s.o.), 7, Clive Street, Alnwick. *26.7.1875:* David Mackenley (s.o.), Alnwick, acquired 16/64ths. *14.8.1875:* Davison transferred 4/64ths to Andrew Richardson (s.o.), Amble, and 8/64ths to Thomas Richards (s.o.), Cornwall.

During 1877/78 the *Manfred* (Capt. John Smith) made a passage from Samarang to Amsterdam. Samarang was left on 14 November.

She was wrecked on the Lacepede Islands (16°50' S., 122°10' E.), off the north-west coast of Australia, during a hurricane, on 24 January 1879. Her crew were saved and arrived at Geralton, Western Australia, on 7 April.

102   *MARQUESS OF WELLINGTON* (1816-1846)

Brig   99 tons   59·3 x 17·9 x 10·7 feet
1813: Built Gateshead by Jonathan Brown.
Owners. *13.9.1813*: Jonathan Brown, Gateshead. *5.1.1814:* George Hawks & William Stanley, London, and Robert Shafto Hawks & John Hawks, Gateshead, all iron merchants. *21.5.1816:* Thomas Annett (m.t.) & George Gibb (m.m.), both Alemouth. Three days later George Gibb became sole owner. *17.11.1825:* Thomas Annett (32/64) & Edward Gibb (Administrator of George Gibb), both Alemouth. *9.7.1830:* Edward Gibb became sole owner following death of Thomas Annett.
Master. *17.11.1825:* Edward Gibb jun.

Described in the *Newcastle Journal* of 12 December 1835 as the *Marquess of Wellington* of Alnmouth (formerly of Berwick), she had: "struck on Alnmouth Bar while leaving harbour and continued beating all that tide. After discharging part cargo was got into harbour with keel and several floors broke."

On the night of 16 July 1840, when on passage from Bangor to Alnmouth, the *Marquess of Wellington* was sailing through the Sound of Islay (about two or three miles south of Portaskaig) when she struck upon something: "where the captain knew from experience there were no sunken rocks." Pieces of timber began floating alongside; a leak developed. Vigourous pumping kept the water at bay and the *Marquess* was able to get home safely. She had struck the wreck of a large American vessel which had foundered some years previously.

On 2 July 1846 the *Marquess* became the property of Isabella Moncur, a spirit dealer & grocer, of Princess Street, Dundee, and was transferred there soon after.

103   *MARTLET* (1864-1868)   O/N 44455

Barque   302 tons   112·6 x 26·3 x 16·6 feet
1862: Built Sunderland by J. Haswell.
Owners. *6.3.1862*: James Ayr (s.o.), Sunderland. *15.8.1862:* Ayr transferred 10/64ths to John Haswell (s.b.), and 5/64ths each to William Salisbury Harrison & Andrew Harrison, all of Sunderland. *7.4.1864:* John Glover (s.br.) London, and on the same day to Robert Hedley (m.m.), Amble. *13.8.1864:* Hedley transferred 24/64ths to Joseph Benbrick Foley (s.br.), 8/64ths to John Hubbard (hoop merchant), and 4/64ths to Alexander Nicholson (broker), all of London.

On 23 March 1868 the *Martlet* was lost off Gallipoli.

104   *MARY* (1831-1836)

Sloop   50 tons   51·5 x 15·5 feet
1800: Built Howden Dike, Yorkshire.
P/R: Whitby (1825/93).
Owners. *23.8.1831:* Sold by Christopher Thompson, Whitby, to John Shanks (salt maker), Amble. *5.9.1831:* John Cowans (pitman), Acklington, acquired 20/64ths and George Smith, Fogston, 24/64ths.

On 10 August 1836 the *Mary* was transferred to Berwick registry when acquired by

John Railson, a North Sunderland (Seahouses) shipowner. He sold her on 15 March 1838 to Robert Smith, a Monkwearmouth master mariner.

The *Mary* was lost on 31 December 1855.

105   *MARY* (?1825-1833)
Sloop   70 tons   53·2 x 18 x 5·5 feet
1805: Built Dundee.
P/R: Berwick (1808/8)
Owners. *25.7.1825:* Henry Wilkinson (16/64, corn merchant), Alnmouth; John Appleby (32/64, corn merchant), Low Buston; John Wilkinson (16/64, corn merchant), High Buston.
Master. *25.7.1825:* George Johnson. *1.10.1837:* Henry Hedley.

The *Mary* was lost on 8 October 1833.

106   *MARY ANN* (1845-1848)
Schooner   71 tons   59·8 x 19 x 7·8 feet
1831: Built Sunderland by Michael McDonnald.
Owners. *12.4.1831:* George Garth (s.w.), Monkwearmouth *9.4.1832:* Matthew Bailes (ship keeper), Sunderland, acquired 32/64ths. *10.5.1836:* Joseph Hodgson (32/64), Crofton, & Thomas Young (32/64, m.m.), Blyth. *7.4.1840:* Following death of Thomas Young his 32/64ths administered by his wife, Mary *4.5.1840:* Mary Young transferred 24/64ths to Joseph Hodgson. *27.8.1845:* Sold by John Hodgson, Crofton Mills, & Mary Young, Blyth, to Edward Thew jun. (s.o.), Lesbury Mills.

On 4 November 1848 the *Mary Ann* was sold to Bolton Stafford, a Blyth shipowner. He had her until re-registered at Yarmouth on 26 April 1850.

107   *MARY'S & ANN* (1831-1855)   O/N 9191
Schooner   98 tons   64 x 19 x 20·8 feet
1831: Built Charlestown, Fife.
Owners. *16.11.1831:* John Mattison (16/64, m.m.), Edward Gibb (16/64, m.m.) & Joseph Simpson (16/64, grocer), all Alnmouth; John Chatwood (16/64, druggist), London.
Masters. *16.11.1831:* John Mattison. *16.6.1838:* Ralph Pattison. *3.4.1839* Thomas Hogg. *9.2.1841:* James Thompson. *14.4.1842:* John Dagliesh. *26.4.1848:* John Lindsay. *2.5.1850:* John Muras. *27.2.1855:* John Welch.

The *Mary's & Ann* was transferred to Whitby during 1855.

108   *MEGGIE DIXON* (1873-1891)   O/N 65462
Barque   474 tons   144·7 x 29·5 x 17·9 feet
1873: Built North Hylton, Sunderland, by James Gardner.
Owners. *6.5.1873:* Andrew Richardson (32/64, s.o.,m.o.), Amble, & Isaac Crane Mann (32/64, m.m.), North Shields. *25.3.1876 share distribution:* Andrew Richardson (14/64), Amble; Crane Mann (24/64), North Shields; David McKenley (8/64, builder), Alnwick; Margaret Tweddle (1/64), Birmingham; Robert Thompson (3/64), Warkworth; Matthew Dixon (3/64, miller), Howick Mill; Robert Elsdon Brown (3/64, deputy coroner of Morpeth), Morpeth; Thomas Green (8/64, confectioner), North Shields. *22.11.1887 share distribution:* David McKenley (8/64) & Ellen Archbold Taylor (2/64), both Alnwick; Elizabeth Mary Turnbull (3/64), Francis Henderson (3/64) & Ann Murray (2/64), all North Shields; Margaret Tweddle (1/64), Birmingham; Robert Thompson (3/64), Warkworth; Matthew Dixon (3/64), Howick Mill; James McDonald (16/64), St Margarets Hope; Mary Brown (3/64), Morpeth; Thomas Smith Howitt (9/64), Dunoon; Robert Middlemass (8/64). *19.9.1887:* Middlemass transferred his 8/64ths to George Simpson (chemist), Alnwick.

The *Meggie Dixon's* maiden voyage took her to the Dutch East Indies under the command of Isaac Crane Mann. Much of her early career was spent trading (apparently very profitably) to this area. Here are some of the freights she earned in 1875:

Java to Bristol £2,457·69p

Newport to Colombo £903·75p

During 1877 she earned £894.17p on a passage from Sunderland to Padang. It was a voyage which was to gain her terrible noteriety because of the neglect, ill treatment and ultimate drowning of one of her apprentices Charles Ashley Cooper details of which have previously been given. On one of her later voyages the *Meggie Dixon* (Capt. McDonald) left London with a cargo of railway sleepers for Algoa Bay (Port Elizabeth). At six o'clock on the morning of 13 September 1880 her fore-mast head was carried away with all its attached gear. She had to put into Falmouth for repairs.

Her British registration was closed on 28 September 1891 following purchase by J. Lorho, of Vannes, France, who re-named her *Gertrude*. In 1893 she was sold to Chargeurs Reunis, a well known French shipping company, for use as a pontoon.

109 ***MENDORA*** O/N 22366

Brigantine 158 tons 84.3 x 21.9 x 12.6 feet

1846: Built Souris, Prince Edward Island.

P/R: Shoreham (23.10.1862).

Owners. 24.10.1862: Robert Lawn (s.o.) & William George Clark (butcher), both Hartlepool. 6.7.1863: Clark became sole owner. 10.5.1875: William George Clark jun., became sole owner.

The *Mendora* is listed in *Amble & District* by T.L. McAndrew as belonging to H. Andrews (Broomhill Coal Co.), Amble, but the facts in her Custom House Register do not bear this out. She was heavily mortgaged to people living in Middlesborough, Stockton and Hartlepool. On 24 September 1877 Henry Foxton Craggs (s.b.), Middlesborough, and George Craggs (timber Merchant), Stockton, transferred what was described as "Mortgage B" to Hugh Andrews for £700 plus interest. Throughout this, and a number of similar transactions, William George Clark jun., of Hartlepool, remained her managing owner.

During 1878/79 she made passages from Amble to London, Rotterdam and Boulogne under the command of Captains Miles and Pringle. On 15 December 1881 the *Mendora* (Capt. Lewis) was wrecked near the Yarmouth Roads when homeward bound from Boulougne.

110 ***MENTOR*** (1857-1859) O/N 23710

Brig 141 tons 74·2 x 21·8 x 13·4 feet

1853: Built Arbroath.

P/R: Arbroath (1850/3)

Owners. *7.2.1857:* John Muras (17/64, m.m.), Amble; Ralph Potts (20/64, blacksmith), Durham; John Henderson (20/64) & Richard Stamp (7/64), both Widrington farmers.

The *Mentor* was reported "lost" on 13 September 1859.

111 ***MUTLAH*** (1877) O/N 17775

Ship 689 tons 157·5 x 32·2 x 20·2 feet

1856: Built Southwick, Sunderland, by W. Petrie.

P/R: London (1864/191).

Owner. *31.1.1877:* John Marshall Henderson (s.o.), Amble.

On 14 April 1877 the *Mutlah* (Capt. Thomas James Farquhar) left Liverpool with a cargo of coal for Bombay. Two days later, in heavy weather, she touched what was thought to be either the Tuscar rocks or Blackwater Bank. Holed and leaking badly an unsuccesful attempt was made to run for Dublin. Driven inshore her anchors were let go off Courtown, on the coast of Wexford, but they did not hold and she came ashore onto some rocks at Glynn. A rocked was fired from the shore, a line straddled the stricked ship, but so quickly was she breaking up that there was nothing to attach it to. The jollyboat was launched with seven men. It capsized, only a man named Hammer made it to the shore. A second boat shared the same fate as the jolly boat; two of its crew were saved - the carpenter Robert Lambert and an able seaman, Peter Lindholm. The Second Mate, Richard Simpson, and steward Robert Bell Archibald made it direct to the shore. Five survivors out of a crew of eighteen.

112   *NELLY* (?1826-1831)
Brig   142 tons   74·4 x 21·5 feet
1812: Built Blyth.
P/R: Berwick (1816/8).
Owners. *13.1.1826:* Edward Gibb (16/64, m.m.), Thomas Annett (16/64, corn merchant), Elizabeth Atkinson (16/64, widow), Elizabeth Fenwick (8/64, widow) & Ann Fenwick (8/64, spinster), all Alnmouth.
Masters: *13.1.1826:* John Thompson. *19.5.1826*: Edward Taylor. *9.3.1831* Anthony Newton.
On 8 April 1831 the *Nelly* was sold to William Gallon & John Hart of South Shields. Gallon becasme sole owncr on 12 July 1836. He was followed by the following owners:
        10.6.1841: Richard Snowdon, Louth.
        1.1.1844: William & Matthew Gallon, South Shields & London.
        26.1.1860: Joseph Prior & Thomas Scott, South Shields.
        8.1.1866: Prior became sole owner.
On 22 March 1869, when bound from the Tyne towards Wisbeach with manure, the *Nelly* stranded at Dimlington and was left with only her masts showing above the water. She was soon broken up by the heavy sea. Her crew left in their own boat and got ashore with the assistance of the Spurn life-boat.

113   *NYMPHEN* (1876-1883)   O/N 5486
Brig   196 tons   82·3 x 21·4 x 14·3 feet
1849: Built Sunderland by William Robinson.
Owners. *9.2.1849:* WilliamBurton(s.o.), Monkwearmouth. *29.6.1853:* John Downie (21/64, draper), Newbiggin; William Potts (21/64, m.m.), Crofton, & Elizabeth Darling (21/64, widow), Backworth. *18.4.1855 share distribution*: Sarah Potts (21/64, widow) & Thomas Armstrong (11/64, m.m.), both Blyth; Elizabeth Darling (32/64). *20.10.1876:* Hugh Andrews (s.o.), Amble.
On what was her first voyage as an Amble ship the *Nymphen* (Capt. R. Lewis) left the port on 3 November 1876 bound to Rotterdam and before the year was out had made a run to Bologne. In the following year a voyage was made to Gothenburg.
The *Nymphen* (Capt. R. Coulson) went missing after leaving Amble on 10 December 1883 with a cargo of coal for Boulogne.

114   *OLIVER* (1872-1880)   O/N 65444
Barque   435 tons   139·3 x 29·1 x 17 feet
1872: Built Sunderland by Richard Thompson.
Owners. *5.9.1872:* William & Robert Davison (16/64 each), David McKenley (16/64, builder) & William Wood (16/64, m.m.), all Alnwick. *21.11.1872:* William Davison trans-

William Robertson's old brigantine *Peace* working cargo while lying ashore at Alnmouth sometime between about 1876 (when the church of St John the Baptist, visible in the background, was completed) and 1878 (when the *Peace* was wrecked). (By permission of the Northumberland Record Office)

ferred 4/64ths to George Davison (s.o.), Alnwick, & David McKenley 4/64ths to George Simpson (chemist), Alnwick. *16.9.1876:* William Davison transferred 6/64ths to Abel Schoefield (s.o.), Alnwick.

The *Oliver* was abandoned on 21 January 1880 in a sinking condition.

115   PACIFIC (1855-1857)   O/N 2074
Barque   361 tons   99·3 x 24·2 x 18·3 feet
1846: Built Sunderland by Todd & Brown.
Owners. *2.9.1846*: James Ayre (s.o.), Sunderland. *28.9.1846:* Andrew White, Sunderland. *23.4.1847:* Ralph Hutchinson (32/64, s.o.) & William Hay (32/64, m.t.), Bishopwearmouth. *30.5.1848:* Thomas Stainton (22/64, iron founder), South Shields, & Allan Wilkin (42/64, iron founder), Newcastle. *10.6.1848:* Allan Wilkin transferred 21/64ths to Walter Allan (iron merchant), Tynemouth. *14.12.1848:* Wilkin transferred his remaining 21/64ths to Joseph Brown, Middlesborough. *30.10.1850 share distribution:* Thomas Stainton (43/64) & Walter Allan (21/64). *16.9.1852:* Stainton transferred 21/64ths to James Wilkin (iron merchant), Newcastle. *9.6.1854:* Thomas Stainton became sole owner. *2.5.1855:* Henry Henderson (22/64, postmaster) & Thomas Henderson (21/64, s.o.), both Warkworth; Jane Elizabeth Henderson (21/64, spinster), North Shields.

Before becoming Coquet owned the *Pacific* brought 2,550 quarters of wheat from the Black Sea to Cork in 1854.

She foundered in the Bay of Biscay on 9 January 1857 when on passage from the Tyne to Barcelona. Her crew of thirteen were saved by the snow *William Ash* and landed at Hull.

115·5   PEACE (1872-1878)   O/N 6505
Brig   83 tons   64·2 x 19·2 x 9·5 feet
1874: Reduced to brigantine rig.
1801: Built Yarmouth.
P/R: Yarmouth (1836/75). Registered in Hartlepool.
Owners. *13.2.1871(?):* Williamson Thorpe (fish merchant), Hartlepool. *21.4.1871:* John Winspeare (s.w.), Hartlepool. *26.8.1871:* William June (timber merchant) Hartlepool. *20.2.1872:* William Robertson (timber merchant), Narrowgate Street, Alnwick.

When Yarmouth registered the *Peace* stranded at Hartlepool on 11 February 1871. Two days later her wreck was sold, by J. Graham & Sons, presumably to Williamson Thorpe (q.v.).

Seventy-one years old when she began her career as an Aln ship, the *Peace* brought a number of timber cargoes direct to Alnmouth from Gothenburg, under the command of Capt. Redpath. She usually called at Amble for an outward cargo of coal.

On 25 January 1878 she was sold to John Gilmore, a Liverpool shipbroker and valuer. In the following March a voyage was made from Alnmouth to Amble and then down to Southampton.

The *Peace* ended her long career on 8 November 1878 when she became a total wreck at Basllinskelligs Bay, Ireland.

116   PENOLA (1937-1940)   O/N 163516
ex *Navaho* ex *Alcyon.*
Auxiliary three-masted topsail schooner.   164 gross 80 net tons   106 x 24·1 x 11·6 feet
Engines . Twin screw, 50 h.p. Junker Diesel.
1908: Built at Kerity-Paimpol, France, by E. Bonne.
Registered in London.

The *Penola* lying in a drydock, probably somewhere on the Tyne, in the 1930's. Her rigging is set up by deadeyes-and-lanyards, just as the Aln and Coquet ships would have been fifty and more years before. Her bow appears to be sheathed for ice navigation, a reminder of her Antarctic exploration days.

(Courtesy: Southy Shields Library)

Owners.1908: J. Libouban, Tréguier, France. *1932:* British owners. *1934*: John Riddoch Rymill, South Australia. *1937:* Fountains Northumberland Trust (W.E. Ruddick, manager.), Amble.

The *Penola* began life as the *Alycon* - one of a large fleet of wooden sailing ships use by French owners right up until World War Two for fishing on the Grand Banks of Newfoundland.

It was reported that she had been sold to British owners in 1932. It might have been at this time that her name was changed to *Navahoe*. A couple of years later John Riddoch Rymill, an Australian who had participated in a number of expeditions to Greenland, found her lying at St Malo. Rymill was looking for a ship to serve with an expedition he was planning to British Graham Land in the Antarctic. The *Navaho* ex *Alcyon* was purchased for £3,000 and re-named *Penola*, after Rymill's estate in South Australia.

The *Penola's* bow was strengthened for navigation in the ice. Her hold was cross-braced but only the foreward part of the hull was sheathed due to lack of funds. On 10 September 1934 she left the United Kingdom bound for Port Stanley, Falkland Islands, under the command of R.E.D. Ryder who with the engineer were the only professionals on board. All the remainder were amateurs. At Port Stanley her rig was altered to make it more suitable for conditions in the Antarctic. The voyage from the Falklands to Port Lockroy, on the coast of Graham Land, was made mainly under sail due to the engines becoming misaligned.

The achievements of what is now referred to as the British Graham Land Expedition included surveys by sledge and aircraft of the coast of West Graham Land and its outlying islands from the Palmer Archipelago to southern Alexander Land as well as penetrating down King George VI Sound to 72° South with sledging parties.

On 12 March 1937 the *Penola* left Graham Land for home. Calling at Stromness, South Georgia, from where she took 67 days to the Azores. The best run was 1,276 miles made in seven days. Falmouth was reached on 4 August. Rymill later published a book about the expedition entitled *Southern Lights* .

Her connection with the Coquet began in 1937 when she was acquired by Fountains Northumberland Trust Ltd., which had been founded by Lt. Commander and Lady Vyner, Fountains Hall, York shire, to help relieve the unemployment prelevant in the North East at that time. They set up offices at Amble to manage the ship and a local firm (Swarland Sawmills & Joinery Ltd.) got the job of enlarging her hatches for cargo work. Mr. J.N. Bank of Newcastle, writing in the *Sea Breezes* magazine of September 1938, describes how he went to Amble to see the *Penola*: "I arrived at Amble ... to find her warping out. She is a very able vessel, and it is interesting to note that she now carries her topsail yards, by request of the crew, who, I learnt, were all local fishermen and had no experience in a ship of this type". He goes on to explain that she was bound to Ullapool with a cargo of bricks. The passage took 13 days. It appears that she made some voyages from Ullapool with grain for a flour mill at Guyzance.

The *Penola* was declared a constructive total loss in 1940 when, on 1 November, she had to be beached following a collision in the Firth of Clyde. A unique vessel in many ways, she was the last active commercial sailing ship to be owned in the North-East.

117   *PERCY* (1855-1876)   O/N 7639
Snow   124 tons   79·9 x 20·3 x 12·6 feet
1855: Built Sunderland by H. Carr.
Owners. *27.11.1855:* James Shotton (20/64, s.o.), Amble; John Shotton (11/64, shoe maker), Warkworth; Robert Green (11/63, s.o.), Togston; John Henry Barry (11/64, m.m.) & John Barry (11/64, s.o.), both Whitby. *30.11.1868:* Green transferred his 11/64ths to Donald

McInnes (m.t.), Amble. *8.3.1869:* John Henry Barry & John Barry transferred their 22/64ths to James Shotton. *19.4.1875:* Donald McInnes died.

During 1870/71 the *Percy* made traded regularly to Boulogne under the command of R. Hart. On 18 December 1876 she was sold to Dixon Stephenson, a Sunderland butcher. He had her for a year after which she was sold to Albert Kent, John Kent sen., John Kent jun. & Richard Bennett Roseveer, all of Mevagissey.

The *Percy* was lost off Bardsey Island on 28 October 1880.

118 ***PERSEVERANCE*** (1852-1876)   O/N 22014
Barque   293 tons   99 x 22·8 x 15·7 feet
31.7.1852: Launched at Amble from yard of Thomas Leighton.
Owners. *9.8.1852:* James Sanderson (24/64, builder), Isabella Sanderson (24/64, spinster) & Thomas Leighton (16/64), all Amble. *21.6.1859:* James Sanderson died; his 24/64ths transferred to Isabella Sanderson.
Masters. *9.8.1852:* Thomas Leighton. *4.2.1854:* John Skury.

On 29 February 1876 the *Perseverance* was transferred to Edwin Spence Roberts, a London shipowner. A couple of weeks later her British registration was closed and D. van de Meyden of Harlingen became owner.

119 ***PORTIA*** (1861-1873)
Brig   212 tons   106·1 x 24 x 14·6 feet
1852: Built Arbroath.
P/R: Dundee (1854/34).
Owner. *22.3.1861:* George John Stanton (m.m.), Alnmouth.

The *Portia* was reported to have foundered on 17 December 1873.

120 ***PRINCE OF SAXE COBOURG*** (1844-1845)
Brig   89 tons   63·7 x 19·4 x 10·3 feet
1819: Built Ramsgate.
P/R: London (1844/218).
Owners. *2.8.1844:* Thomas Brown (s.o.), Amble.
Master. *2.8.1844:* John Phillips.

On 3 May 1845 the *Prince of Saxe Cobourg* was sold to William Boutland (s.b.), of Bill Quay. He was succeeded by the following North-East owners: *9.4.1846:*Gilbert Henderson (56/64, m.m.), Robert Urwin (8/64, butcher), Newcastle. *20.2.1851:* Henderson transferred 24/64ths to Thomas Wilkin (m.t.), Newcastle. *11.1.1858:* David Baxter & Matthew Storm, Whitby.

During April 1864, when bound from the Tyne to Havre, she put into Lowestoft with bow stove, bowsprit and main-yard broken following a collision with the *Catherine Tucker* (Callao to Leith). From Havre she came back to the Tyne in 13 days.

On 7 December 1867, on passage from the Tyne to London, the *Prince of Saxe Cobourg* (Capt. Watson) went ashore near Cleethorpes and became a total wreck.

121 ***PROSPECT*** (1849-1861)   O/N 15416
Schooner   132 tons   77·5 x 23·3 x 12 feet
1846: Built Sunderland by H. Dobbinson.
P/R: Sunderland (1846/144).
Owners. *29.1.1849:* George Potter (24/64, m.m.), Robert Simpson (24/64, agent) & Henry George Gibb (16/64), all Alnmouth. *2.2.1860:* Following death of Henry George Gibb, his 16/64ths to Eliza Gibb (widow), Alnmouth.

On 2 January 1861 the *Prospect* (Capt. Darling) sprang a leak when on passage from Amble to France with coal. She put back into the Coquet Roads, anchored, and was then abandoned just before going down. Her wreck later drifted ashore at Alnmouth where it was put up for sale.

122   **PROTESTOR** (1855-1866)   O/N 2843
Brig   190 tons   82·5 x 25·5 x 14·8 feet
1839: Built Sunderland by R. Young.
Owners: *5.12.1855:* John Duncan (19/64, s.o.), Amble; Robert Davison & David Mackinley (19/64 each), both Alnwick; Thomas Brown (7/64, m.m.), Clay, Norfolk. *21.7.1857:* Brown transferred his 7/64ths to Luke Richardson (joiner), Willington.
    During December 1866 the *Protestor* became waterlogged and was abandoned in the North Sea.

123   **PROVIDENCE** (1855-1866)   O/N 24533
Snow   194 tons   89 x 20 x 12·9 feet
1855: Built Amble by James Sanderson & Thomas Leighton.
Owners. *7.4.1855:* James Sanderson (8/64, s.b.), Thomas Leighton (8/64, s.b.), Isabella Sanderson (8/64, spinster) & James Smith (16/64, m.m.), all Amble; George Thompson (8/64, postman), Warkworth; William Leighton (16/64, m.m.), Liverpool. *25.2.1860 share distribution:* Thomas Leighton (4/64), George Thompson (8/64), Isabella Sanderson (8/64) & James Smith (16/64); James Nairn (12/64, stonemason), Amble; Martin Fleming (m.m.) & Luke Hurst (agent, jointly 16/64), both Liverpool.
Master. *7.4.1855:* Robert Richardson.
    In 1858 the *Providence* (Capt. Chisholm) arrived at Peterhead at the end of a 44 day, heavy weather passage from Archangel during which she had lost her bowsprit.
    On 29 November 1861 she left Amble for Boulogne under the command of Capt. Adler. When off Blyth a heavy squall sprung one of her topmasts. It was decided to run back to the Coquet Roads where, just as she brought up, the fore-mast went by the board taking with it the main topmast. With only the main lowermast standing, she was brought into Amble by the tug *Ellen Browne*. The *Providence* was wrecked at Boulogne on 13 January 1866.

124   **PULTENEY** (1840-1849)
Schooner   50 tons   52 x 15·5 x 8·9 feet
1804: Built Bridport, Dorset.
P/R: Exeter (1837/35)
Owners. *25.10.1839:* Sold by William Pitts, Dawlish, to Henry Nelson, Starcross, Devon. *12.11.1839:* Samuel Davidson (m.m.), Newcastle. *2.7.1840:* Robert Davidson (brewer), Alnwick, acquired 32/64ths.
Masters. *28.11.1839:* Samuel Davidson. *10.2.1844:* George Smith. *9.4.1844:* Samuel Davidson. *13.2.1847:* William Scott. *6.3.1847:* Samuel Davidson. *7.10.1848:* John Mallock. *27.3.1849:* Samuel Davidson.
    On 5 July 1849 the *Pulteney* was transferred to Leith registration.

125   **RACHEL** (1825-1846)
Sloop   32 tons   40 x 14 x 7·6 feet
1825: Built North Shields.
Owners. *10.5.1825:* John Skelly (32/64, farmer), Denwick, & Richard Robson (32/64, farmer), Alnwick.

Masters. *10.3.1831:* George Gray. *20.6.1838:* Thomas Thompson. *30.5.1844:* Thomas Brown. *1.5.1841:* Henry Gray. *5.4.1851:* John Greenfield. *7.7.1851:* Thomas Milne.

Following the death of John Skelly, the *Rachel* was acquired by Henry Gray of North Sunderland, on 6 May 1846. He sold her to John Stewart, a Newcastle master mariner, on 23 September 1850.

On 21 July 1851, when on passage from North Sunderland to Dundee, she went ashore while entering that port and became a total wreck. Her crew were saved.

126	*RADIANT* (1848-1876)		O/N 18639

Snow   222 tons   86·8 x 22·1 x 14·8 feet
1848: Built Blyth by Bowman & Drummond.
Owners. *19.4.1848:* George, Robert & Andrew Richardson (16/64 each), all Amble ship-owners; John Gibson (16/64, s.o.), Blyth. *12.4.1854 share distribution:* George (21/64), Robert (21/64) & Andrew (22/64) Richardson.
Masters. *19.4.1848:* John Gibson. *13.4.1854:* John Smith.

The *Radiant's* Custom House Register notes that she foundered Between Bergen & the Naze of Norway on about 29 November 1876.

127   *RAMBLER* (1844-1849)
Schooner   111 tons   67 x 17·8 x 11·4 feet
1842: Built South Stockton.
P/R: Stockton (1842/40)
Owners. *13.3.1847:* Sold by Thomas Hopper, Stockton, to Robert Simpson (24/64, agent), Henry George Gibb (12/64, m.m.), Robert Bain (8/64, m.m.), Margaret Simpson (12/64, widow) & Henry Hindmarch (8/64, blacksmith), all Alnmouth.
Master: *23.3.1847:* Robert Bain.

During December 1849 the *Rambler* disappeared with all hands. She had last been seen in Bridlington Bay.

128	*RED DEER* (1875-1880)		O/N 47387

Ship   693 tons   162 x 32·5 x 19·5 feet
1863: Built Ardrossan by Barr & Shearer.
P/R: London (1864/495).
Owners: *1865:* Adamson & Co., London. *19.8.1875:* John Marshall Henderson (s.o.,m.o.), Amble. *31.3.1876:* James Robert Laing, St Leonards, Sussex, acquired 28/64ths.

In her early days, as a London owned ship, the *Red Deer* had been employed in the China trade.

On 16 November 1877, when on passage from Sunderland towards Padang, she put into the Tyne, after ten days at sea, with some of her crew refusing duty. They were charged at South Shields Police Court with refusing to obey the lawful commands of the master - Capt. Meehap.

Thomas Brock, a Glasgow timber merchant, became owner on 10 December 1880 and she was transferred to that port twelve months later.

The *Red Deer* was abandoned at sea when on passage from Baltimore towards Havana on 27 February 1886.

129	*REGALIA* (1862-1867)		O/N 26195

Snow   156 tons   91 x 21·6 x 12·4 feet
1859: Built Sunderland by S.P. Austin.
Owners. *15.2.1862:* Thomas Leighton (33/64, s.o.), George Hall (27/64, s.o.) & Francis Chi-

sholm (4/64, m.m.), all Amble. *10.3.1862:* Leighton transferred 6/64ths to Edward Adler (m.m.), Amble.

The *Regalia* was transferred to Yarmouth registration (No. 53) in 1867. For some time she was owned by W. Bullard of that port before returning to the North-East Coast when acquired by William Allhusen, a Newcastle chemical manufacturer, on 22 February 1889. He was followed by:

13.3.1891: United Alkali Co., Liverpool.
13.2.1903: Tyne Wherry Co., Newcastle.
2.5.1916: John Anderson (ship repairer), Felling.
3.5.1916: Tyne Iron Shipbuilding Co., Willington Quay.

Her register was not closed until 29 November 1920. By then she was described as a "hulk," a role which I suspect she had acted for many years.

130 **ROBERT & MARGARET** (1825-1839)
Sloop   54 tons   49·9 x 26·3 x 7·3 feet
1791: Built North Shields.
P/R: Berwick (1806/5)
Owners. *22.12.1825:* Robert Young (22/64, wharfinger), Alnmouth; Edward Thew (21/64) & Ralph Smith (21/64, m.t.), both Alnwick. *31.3.1827:* Smith transferred his 21/64ths to Thew & Young who then had 32/64ths each. *13.7.1830:* Following the death of Robert Young his 32/64ths were transferred to William McDougal, Alnwick, in trust for John Young, Alnwick, who became owner of them on 1.3.1836.
Masters. *22.12.1825:* George Stanton. *14.11.1827:* Robert Gibb. *5.8.1830:* James Moddril. *1.7.1831:* Robert Margent. *13.1.1832:* George Johnson. *27.12.1832:* George Swan. *4.3.1835:* Joseph Davison. *13.2.1836:* Daniel Whiteman.

The *Robert & Margaret's* register was cancelled on 24 June 1839.

131 **ROSELLA** (1869-1880)   O/N 27369
Barque   283 tons   111·7 x 26·4 x 16·4 feet
1859: Built Sunderland by James Briggs.
Owners. *22.7.1859:* Matthew Hall Atkinson (s.o.), North Shields. *25.5.1869:* John Henry Barry (s.o.), Amble.

On 23 February 1860, when bound from Odessa to Glasgow, the *Rosella* put into Cadiz in a damaged condition after being in collision with the Glasgow schooner *Robina* off Cape St. Vincent. The *Robina* was abandoned in a sinking state; her crew were picked up by the *Rosella*. During 1863 she made a 146 day passage from Foochow to Deal - 57 days from St. Helena.

On 19 March 1880 the *Rosella* became a wreck after stranding at St. Annes, Guadeloupe.

132 **ST GEORGE** (1854)   O/N 25650
Brig   126 tons   70·4 x 18 x 11·9 feet
1833: Built St Georges Cove, Gaspe, Lower Canada.
P/R: Jersey (1849/5)
Owners. *26.1.1854:* Sold by William Bisson, Jersey, to Thomas Walker, Amble.

When Jersey owned, the *St George* was driven ashore at Amble during a severe east-south-east gale on 7 January 1854. Refloated, she became Amble owned for little more than a month before being acquired by James Wilkie of Blyth. On 5 June 1854 Wilkie transferred 16/64ths to James Heron, a Blyth shipowner, and 32/64ths to William Heslop (innkeeper),

76

Sarah of Seaton Sluice Capt. Stephen Oxley

Photograph of a painting of the snow *Sarah* by the Hamburg artist F.T Albinus when she was owned in Seaton Sluice and commanded by
Stephen Oxley. Notice the fore-topmast and main-topgallant studding sails. The try-sail mast, which distinguishes the snow rig from the brig,
can be clearly seen abaft the main lower-mast.

Newcastle. The *St George* was re-registered at Greenock on 16 Novemner 1855.

133   **SAPPHO** (1860-1861)   O/N 36423
Brig   180 tons   97 x 22·3 x 12·9 feet
1859: Built West Cape, Prince Edward Island.
Owners. *20.1.1860:* Sold by James Colledge Pope, Prince Edward Island, to James Smith (m.m.), Amble.

On 27 December 1861 the *Sappho* was wrecked near Saffi (Safi [Asfi]), Morocco.

134   **SARAH** (1814-1819)(1825-1827)   O/N 2099
Snow   227 tons   88·6 x 25·2 x 15·5 feet
Capacity: 360 tons coal, 278 tons tallow, 40 tons ballast.
1814: Built Sunderland by Thomas Burn.
Owners. *26.10.1814:* Robert Fenwick, Alemouth, James Hardy (m.t.), Alnwick, & Isaac Henderson (m.m.), Sunderland. *11.3.1819:* James Straker (s.o.), North Shields, & Thomas Ward (s.o.), Bridlington. *22.11.1825:* James David (21/64, farmer), Weedside, Robert Fenwick (21/64), Warkworth, & James Hardy (21/64, m.t.), Alnwick. *1.5.1827:* Stephen Oxley (48/64, m.m.) & Thomas Tindal (16/64, pot maker), both Seaton Sluice. *7.7.1846:* John Robert Kelso (48/64, s.o.), North Shields; Philip & Ann Taylor (8/64 each), Seaton Sluice. *27.9.1850:* Kelso became sole owner. *18.10.1850:* William Pyle jun. (s.b.), Sunderland. *25.11.1850:* Leonard Eden & George Bird (32/64 each), both South Shields. *27.2.1854:* George Brown Purvis (s.o.), North Shields.
Masters. *7.7.1846:* James Cowans. *21.10.1850:* John Galley. *29.11.1850:* Hugh Rendell. *3.3.1854:* Robert Lowrey. *8.3.1854:* Thomas Harrison.

On 10 March 1857, when on passage from London to the Tyne, the *Sarah* ran ashore Tetney Haven. She was refloated the following day and towed into Grimsby.

The *Sarah* was lost on the Dutch coast on 20 November 1860 when bound from the Tyne to Schiedam. Her crew were saved.

135   **SARAH** (1829-1832)
Sloop   40 tons   43 x 14 feet
1828: Built Aberdeen
Owner. *18.7.1829:* Ralph Wake (m.m.), Alnmouth.
Master. *18.7.1829:* Ralph Wake.

On 23 April 1832 the *Sarah* was transferred to Aberdeen.

136   **SARAPTA** (1864-1870)   O/N 49742
Brig   203 tons   96·5 x 25 x 13·8 feet
1864: Built Sunderland by Gray & Young.
Owners. *7.5.1864:* George Richardson (16/64, s.o.) & William Henry Schollar (16/64, m.m.), both Amble; David McKenzie (16/64) & Robert Davison (16/64), both Alnwick shipowners.

On 22 December 1870 the *Sarepta* (Capt. Mann), when homeward bound from Boulogne, was wrecked at Tod head, Near Stonehaven, Kincardine. Her master and two seamen were drowned.

137   **SAVANNAH LA MAR** (1863-1869)   O/N 20129
Brig   255 tons   107·8 x 23·4 x 14·9 feet
1857: Built Alloa.
P/R: Liverpool.

Owners.*1857 L/R:* A. King, Glasgow. *1861 L/R:* Friend & Co., Liverpool. *30.7.1863:* Thomas Turnbull (32/64, s.o.) & Isaac Crane Mann (16/64, m.m.), both Amble; Edmund Hannay Watts jun., & William Milburn (jointly 16/64), both Blyth shipbrokers.

On 19 September 1869 the *Savannah la Mar* was wrecked on the Scaw Reef, at the entrance to the Kattegat, when on passage from Cronstadt to London with a cargo of wheat..

138   *SEAFLOWER* (1854-1876)   O/N 26418
Schooner   146 tons   79 x 21 x 12·5 feet
1849: Built Sunderland by R.H. Potts & Bros.
Owners. *15.10.1849:* Robert Hutton Potts & Hutton Potts (jointly 48/64, both ship builders) and George Walton (16/64, m.m.), all Sunderland. *23.11.1854:* Sold by Robert Hutton Potts, Hutton Potts & Lipson Hutton Potts, Sunderland, to James Shotton (20/64, butcher), Amble; Robert Green (9/64, agent), Togston; John Henry Barry (15/64, m.m.) & John Barry (15/64, s.o.), both Whitby.
Masters. *29.11.1854:* Thomas Atkinson. *26.3.1855:* John Claxton.

On 12 January 1864, when bound from Boulogne towards the Coquet, the *Seaflower* struck Cross Sand, off Caister. Making a lot of water she was run ashore on Winterton Beach. Some local boatmen got her re-floated and taken into Yarmouth for £147·10. She was still running in the Boulogne trade in the early 1870's under the command of R. Adler.

The *Seaflower* was sold to George Judson (32/64), a Seaham shipowner, and Joseph Milmer (32/64), a butcher of Southwick, Sunderland, on 11 October 1876.

Under the command of a Capt. Foggin she left Seaham, on what was to be her last voyage, on 14 November 1878 and almost immediately ran into a severe gale which drove her ashore at Cleethorpes. Her crew were taken off by lifeboat. The wreck was burnt.

139   *SIR HENRY WEBB* (1845-1848)
Brig   223 tons   84·4 x 22·8 x 14·3 feet
1845: Built Sunderland by Todd & Brown.
Owners. *12.6.1845:* Thomas Browne, Amble. *15.6.1845:* Charles Burnett (m.m.), acquired 3/64ths. *13.2.1847:* Browne again became sole owner. *28.12.1847:* James Bainbridge, Lumley Thicks, Durham, acquired 3/64ths.
Masters. *12.6.1845:* Charles Burnett. *24.6.1848:* Thomas Hopper.

On 29 June 1848 the *Sir Henry Webb* was transferred to London.

140   *SIR JOHN RENNIE* (1845-1848)
Brig   203 tons   79·7 x 21·3 x 14·2 feet
1845: Built Sunderland by Edward Brown.
Owners. *12.2.1845:* Thomas Browne (56/64), Amble; John Murdock (8/64), Bishopwearmouth.
Masters. *12.1.1845:* John Murdock. *6.5.1847:* Thomas Steward. *4.2.1848:* Thomas Hopper.

On 1 February 1848 the *Sir John Rennie* was sold to William Tomlin sen., of Limehouse. She was transferred to the London register three months later. *Lloyd's Register* for 1856 gives her owner as J. Harper.

141   *SIR WILLIAM WALLACE* (1859-1866)   O/N 32892
Brig   165 tons   81·2 x 23·4 x 14·1 feet
1835: Built Aberdeen by Alexander Hall & Sons. Cost £1,500.
P/R: London (1835/26).
Owners. *18.4.1859:* John Temple (m.m.), Warkworth. *30.12.1860:* John Temple died; his

widow, Mary Ann Temple, became owner. *10.7.1866:* William Castles (farmer), Warkworth, acquired 26/64ths.

The *Sir William Wallace* stranded at least twice during her career as a Coquet owned ship but was lucky enough to be re-floated each time. The first occassion was on 9 February 1861 when she drove ashore on Ryhope Snook. She had arrived off the Tyne Bar the previous night but had been to late to take the tide. Robert Dowie was master at the time. The second stranding happened the following year when the *Sir William Wallace* struck the Hirtsholmens, near the Scaw Reef, at the entrance to the Kattegat, when on passage from Amble to Cronstadt. Put ashore full of water she was refloated on 24 September and taken into Frederikshavn for repairs.

On 28 November 1863 she arrived at the Caledonian Canal at the end of a 35 day, heavy weather passage from Riga. Bound to Belfast with a cargo of linseed. Her next owners, who acquired her on 17 October 1866, came from a variety of areas in the North-East:

Jonathan Redshaw (13/64, labourer), Cold Rowley.
William Brown (13/64, labourer), West Hartlepool.
Thomas Brown (13/64, labourer), Sheriff Hill.
George Brown (13/64, m.m.), Blyth.
William Redpath (12/64, labourer), Ponteland.

When under their joint ownership she went ashore again on 3 December 1867 this time at Tetney, Lincolnshire. The mainmast went by the board; three anchors and their cables were lost. After being re-floated she was taken to Grimsby for repairs.

The *Sir William* was sold to foreigners on 13 November 1874. The *Newcastle Daily Journal* of 12 July 1876 reported that: "the brig *Sir William Wallace* was yesterday arrested at Middlesbrough under a warrent from the Court of Admiralty for colourably assuming the Belgian flag with a view to avoid the interference of the Board of Trade under the Merchant Shipping Act, 1873." What happened was that her British registry was reopened on 26 October 1876 when Edward Jopling of Sunderland acquired her. George Brown of Blyth, a previous part owner, was manager for a few months before James Saunders took over the job.

She ended her catalouge of near disasters by going missing after sailing from Seaham on 22 October 1882.

142   *SPECULATION* (1850-1853)
Schooner   93 tons   65 x 17·5 x 10·1 feet
1807: Built Redbridge, Southampton.
Owners. *6.4.1850:* George Hall (s.o.), Amble.
Masters. *6.4.1850:* Robert Rochester. *24.3.1852:* Robert Hedley.

On 8 February 1853 the *Speculation* was sold to George Stanisland Touache, a Bishopwearmouth master mariner. He had her until 6 March 1854 when Dixon Stephenson, a Sunderland butcher, became owner.

She was re-registered at Leith on 10 March 1855.

143   *STAR OF PEACE* (1880 -1887)   O/N 49765
Brig   235 tons   103·1 x 25 x 14·7 feet
1865: Built Sunderland by J. Blumer.
Owners. *12.4.1865:* Francis Stafford (16/64, s.o.), William Chambers (12/64, pilot), Edward Morrison (8/64, steam boat owner), Ralph Burn (4/64, s.w.) & George Nicholson (4/64, m.m.), all Blyth; William Rymer (12/64, off putter), Percy Main; Elijah Brooks (8/64, forgeman), Newcastle. *16.2.1869:* Nicholson transferred his 4/64ths to Stafford. *6.12.1870:* Morrison transferred his 8/64ths to Stafford. *10.2.1874:* William Rymer died; his12/64ths

transferred to joint ownership of William & George Rivers, Edinburgh. *7.6.1880:* J. Park, Warkworth, appointed manager by Hugh Andrews, Warkworth.

Before becoming Amble owned the *Star of Peace* made a smart 11 day run from the Tyne to Oporto in 1874. As an Amble ship she was commanded by William Gair and carried coal to Calais, Syra Island, Dieppe, Dunbar, Chatham, Dartmouth, Elsinore and Travemunde. On 22 February 1886 she left Amble bound to Barbados for orders. From Barbados she went to St Lucia to discharge on 13 April.

The *Star of Peace* was wrecked on Amble South Pier when inward bound from Christiania with pit props on 23 December 1887.

144   **STORK** (1878)   O/N 45031
Brig   157 tons   89·3 x 23·4 x 10·9 feet
1840: Built U.S.A.
Registered at London.
Owners. *1875/76 L/R:* C.M. Elkin, London. *1878 L/R:* H. Andrews (Broomhill Coal Co.), Amble.

Before being acquired by Hugh Andrews the *Stork* visited Amble on a number of occasions taking cargoes of coal to Gravesend, Dundee and Harlingen under the command of E. Finney and E. Rowcliff.

On 29 March 1878 she foundered after colliding with the 225 ton South Shields snow *Thomas & Isabella,* twelve miles S.E. by E of Flamborough Head, when on passage from Trouville to Amble in ballast.

145   **SUN** (1861-1874)   O/N 26909
Snow   156 tons   91·2 x 23·2 x 11·2 feet
1855: Built Sunderland by John Barkes.
Owners. *13.3.1855:* Thomas Weir (block & mast maker), Sunderland. *22.2.1861:* Henry Heatley (48/64, s.o.) & Isabella Gibb (16/64, widow), both Alnmouth.

On 16 February 1864 the *Sun* (Capt. Heatley) arrived in the Tyne from Boulogne after experiencing heavy weather. She had had to slip from an anchorage off Old Hartly and was driven out into the North Sea. Three days before making it back to the Tyne, when lying under double reefed topsails about twelve miles east of

146   **SUNDEW** (1863-1886)   O/N 28791
Snow   182 tons   90·4 x 23·9 x 13·4 feet
1860: Built Sunderland by J. Barkes.
Owners. *26.9.1860:* William Hunter Watson (24/64, s.o.), John Hunter Watson (8/64, s.o.) & Richard Hewson Halliday (32/64, m.m.), & all Sunderland. *16.2.1863*: Joseph Harrison (19/64, s.o.), Warkworth; John Henderson (19/64, s.o.) & Edward Gibb (7/64, m.m.), both Amble; Edward Thomas Simpson (19/64, s.o.), Alnmouth. *12.3.1867:* Henderson transferred 19/64ths to Harrison. *21.12.1871:* Harrison transferred 29/64ths to John Henderson and 9/64ths to Edward Gibb. *20.1.1874:* John Henderson died; share distribution became: Edward Thomas Simpson (19/64), Alnmouth; Edward Gibb (16/64), Amble, and 29/64ths jointly by John Woodger (m.f.), Yarmouth, & Thomas Young (s.o.), Amble.

The *Sundew* (Capt. Gibb) made a number of coal runs to Boulogne in the early 1870's.On 23 November 1875 John Turner, Blyth, became managing owner. He was followed on 2 May 1885 by John Cole, also of Blyth, and again on 9 October 1884 by Thomas Jefferson of West Hartlepool.

She was run down and sunk by the Hull steamer *Winstead* , in the Thames, on 24 May 1886.

147 *SUNRISE*
Barque   257 tons
2.7.1859: Launched at Amble from yard of Mr Sanderson.
Owners. *1859 L/R:* Pembroke, London. *1863 L/R:* Elder, London.
   At her launch the *Sunrise* was described as a: "clipper barque intended for the Southern trade." In her time she voyaged to the Falkland Islands. By 1869 she had dropped out of *Lloyd's Register.*

148 *SWIFT* (1815-1835)
Schooner   86 tons   62 x 18·1 feet
1815: Built South Blyth by John Davidson.
Owners. *5.1.1815:* James Thoburn & Frank Marshall, South Blyth rope makers; Henry Wilkinson, High Buston; Robert Weddell & Aaron Smith, Alnwick merchants. *18.7.1825:* Henry Wilkinson (32/64, corn merchant), Alnmouth; John Wilkinson (8/64, corn merchant), High Buston; Aaron Smith & Robert Weddell (8/64ths each), both Alnwick; James Thoburn (8/64, rope maker), South Blyth;
Masters. *18.7.1825:* John Mattison. *30.7.1831:* James Modrel. *7.6.1832:* Huntress.
   On 7 July 1832 the *Swift* was sold to John Huntress (32/64, m.m.), South Shields, & John Robson (32/64, m.m.), North Shields. She was wrecked near Boulogne on 7 October 1835.

149 *TALISMAN* (?1825-1834)
Sloop   68 tons   53·5 x 17·7 feet
1807: Built Pallion, Sunderland, by J. Goodchild jun.
P/R: Berwick (1816/1)
Owners. *16.12.1825:* Edward Threw, Alnwick; Robert Young, Ralph Smith, & John Young, all Alemouth. *3.2.1827:* Smith transferred his 16/64ths to Robert Young, Alemouth. *6.8.1831:* Robert Gibbon (32/64), Warkworth Cottage, & Arthur Gibbon (32/64), Acklington Park.
Masters. *6.8.1831:* James Hay. *17.8.1831:* Joseph Robertson.
   The *Talisman* was wrecked near Aberdeen on 2 April 1834.

150 *TELEMACHUS* (1847-1857)   O/N 25010
Schooner   111 tons   75·6 x 18·8 x 10·6 feet
1802: Built Bideford.
P/R: London (1818/44).
Owners. *19.11.1824:* Alexander Fairweather (cabinet maker), North Shields. *23.4.1839:* Thompson Smith (s.b.), Willington. *29.8.1839:* Edward Whitfield (22/64, agent) Newcastle; Thomas Wraith (21/64, agent), Pelaw; William Johnson (21/64, grocer), Fawdon. *17.12.1847:* Edward Whitfield (s.o.), Amble. *6.4.1849:* John Turnbull (s.o.), Amble, acquired 22/64ths. *23.7.1853 share distribution:* Whitfield (2/64), John Turnbull (50/64) & William Turnbull (14/64, s.o.), all Amble. *26.7.1873 share distribution:* John (22/64), William (14/64) & Thomas (28/64) Turnbull, all Amble shipowners.
   During a severe east-south-east gale which struck the north-east coast in January 1854 the *Telemachus* was driven ashore near Amble along with eight other vessels but later refloated.
   On 13 June 1857 she was sold to Thomas Howard Leaker, William Robert Howard Leaker & John Pearson, of Bristol.

151 **THISTLE** (1829-1831)
Sloop   77 tons   58 x 18 feet
1804: Built Grangemouth.
P/R: Hull (1826/133).
Owners. *25.2.1828*: William John Grey (60/64) & William Grey Marchbank (4/64), both Newcastle shipbuilders. *29.4.1829:* John Shanks (salt manufacturer), Amble. *29.4.1829:* Thomas George Smith (coal owner), Fogston, acquired 24/64ths & Robert Cowans (coal owner), Acklington, 16/64ths. *30.5.1829:* Shanks transferred 8/64ths to Daniel Whiteman (m.m.), Alnmouth. *29.8.1831:* Whiteman transferred 4/64ths each to Shanks & Cowans.
Masters. *29.4.1829:* Daniel Whiteman. *18.8.1831:* George Marshall.
On 16 September 1831 the *Thistle* was transferred to Whitby.

152 **THOMAS RUSBRIDGER** (1867-1869)   O/N 24496
Brig   120 tons   67·4 x 19·1 x 12·1 feet
1847: Built Bill Quay, Gateshead.
P/R: Arundel (17.2.1852).
Owners. *13.1.1855:* Sold by John Pepper & Thomas Cunningham, both Littlehampton ship-owners, to John Bell (marine store dealer), South Shields. *19.1.1855:* James Osbourn (m.m.), South Shields, acquired 21/64ths. *4.2.1861:* William Foster (m.m.), North Shields. *13.7.1867:* George Burn (32/64, m.m.), Amble, & Benjamin Wake (32/64, gardener), Morpeth; George Burn acquired Wake's 32/64ths on same day.
The *Thomas Rusbridger* is supposed to foundered in the North Sea on about 17 October 1869.

153 **TRADER** (1839-1846)
Sloop   48 tons   50 x 16·7 x 7 feet
1839: Built Amble by George Surtees.
Owners. *19.10.1839:* Thomas Brown (22/64), Amble, & John Foster (32/64, agent), Newcastle.
Masters. *19.10.1839:* Richard Wilson. *10.10.1840:* Frederick Mitchell. *18.3.1841:* Robert Richardson. *29.7.1841:* George Stanton. *3.5.1843:* Thomas Charlton. *7.7.1843:* John Phillips. *14.9.1844:* James Phillips. *17.12.1844:* James Straker.
On 17 March 1847 the *Trader* was sold to Andrew Spence jun., of Broughton Ferry, Fife, and transferred to Dundee five weeks later.

154 **TULIP**
Schooner   101 tons   77·3 x 21·5 x 10·6 feet
1867: Built Amble by D.A. Douglas.
Owners. *22.1.1868:* Samuel Tyzack (40/64), William Branfoot (8/64) & William Snowball (16/84), all Sunderland.
On 10 October 1873 the *Tulip* was wrecked on Taunton Sand, Barnstable Bay.

155 **UNION** (1867-1869)   O/N 2995
Snow   156 tons   75 x 22·8 x 13·1 feet
1834: Built Stockton.
P/R: Ipswich.
Owners. *25.12.1860:* William Edward Boutland (s.b.), John George Boutland (s.o.) & Robert Pringle (s.o.), all Bill Quay. *11.5.1861:* William John Brown, Seaham. *3.6.1866:* Samuel Peter Austin & Samuel Peter Austin jun., both Sunderland shipbuilders. *31.1.1866:* Samuel Tyzack, William Branfoot & John Zealand, all Sunderland shipowners. *20.7.1867:* Dennis

Ainsley Douglas, Robert Mather & Andrew Chambers, all Amble; John Douglas, Sunderland; Robert Shout Douglas, Acton Hall, Northumberland. *8.4.1868:* Andrew Chambers became sole owner.

During the November of 1860 the *Union* stranded on the Herd Sand, South Shields. She was then registered in Ipswich. William Edward Boutland, a Tyneside shipbuilder, and a couple of others bought her hull for £125. He had her repaired and re-fitted at his Bill Quay Yard.

The *Union* was lost near the Shipwash, off Orfordness, on 14 February 1869.

156   *UNION PACKET* (1832-1836)
Brig (originally brigantine)   113 tons   66·6 x 20·3 feet
1803: Built Gateshead by Summers & McQueen.
Owners. *27.8.1803:* George Straker (s.o.), Gateshead. *? date:* Transferred to Dunbar (1826/11). *31.5.1832:* Sold by James Rae & Charles Brown, Dunbar, to George Gibb (35/64, m.m.), Warkworth, and Henry Poritt (farmer), Amble.
Masters. *31.5.1832:* George Gibb. *23.1.1834:* Henry Heatly. *22.5.1834:* James Porritt.

On 26 February 1836 the *Union Packet* was sold to John Gibson, a Blyth master mariner. He kept her until 15 April 1850 when Thomas Shotton of Low Cramlington became owner. She was lost on the French Coast, with all hands, on 24 February 1854.

157   *UNION T.* (1874-1879)
Brigantine   198 tons   98·4 x 24·9 x 12·1 feet
1864: Built Saint John, New Brunswick, by Simon Tufts.
Owners. *24.8.1874:* Sold by Simon Tufts & David D. Long, Saint Johns, N.B., to Hugh Andrews (coal owner), Eastfield Hall, Northumberland. *16.11.1875:* Richard Jack, Newcastle, appointed manager.

On what must have been her first voyage for Hugh Andrews the *Union T.* made a ballast passage from Londonderry to Amble under the command of J. Matthews. She then sailed for Bremerhaven on 25 September 1874. In the following year she brought a cargo of hay to Amble from Rotterdam before returning to the Dutch port with coal.

On 23 September 1879 the *Union T* became a total wreck at Newbiggin Point

158   *UNITED* (1882-?1884)   O/N 4315
Brig   90 tons   89·3 x 24 x 14 feet
1851: Sunderland.
P/R: Colchester (1857/5).
Owners. *31.5.1882:* Hugh Andrews, Eastfield Hall, Northumberland. *8.7.1882:* John Park, Warkworth Harbour, appointed manager.

On 2 April 1883 the *United* was sold to Charlotte Burnman, a North Shields widow. Its register was closed on 6 June, in the same year, and endorsed "sold to Germany". She is no longer listed in *Lloyd's Register* after 1885.

159   *VANQUISHER* (1864-1879)   O/N 43731
Snow   233 tons   99·5 x 25·7 x 15·2 feet
1861: Built Hylton, Sunderland, by Green & Richards.
Owners. *8.8.1861:* Thomas Glaholm & Samuel Sinclair, both Sunderland rope makers. *6.4.1864:* James Heatley (s.o.), Blyth. *12.4.1864:* Robert Simpson & George Potter (shipowners), acquired 20/64ths each, and Matthew George Simpson (agent), 4/64ths, all Alnmouth. On 11 December 1879 the *Vanquisher* was sold to Henry Vane, London. He was fol-

lowed, on 17 June 1885, by Henry Booth Vane & William Hammerton Vane, both of Ratcliff, London, who became joint owners. She was broken up in 1887.

160   *VICTORIA* (1882-1887)   O/N 17621
Brigantine   83 tons   64·9 x 19·4 x 10 feet
1839: Built Southwold, Suffolk.
Owner. *31.5.1882:* Hugh Andrews (s.o.), Felton. *3.7.1882:* John Park, Warkworth, appointed manager.

Under the command of Captains Coulson and Mather, the *Victoria* carried coal from Amble to Boulogne, Cuxhaven, Rye, Peterhead and Sheerness between 1882 and 1885..

On 29 January 1887 she was sold to Alexander Langlands, a Montrose shipowner.

161   *VICTORIA* (1853-1855)   O/N 7847
Brig   249 tons   83·6 x 23 x 15·3 feet
1843: Built Black Sod, County of Mayo.
P/R: Galaway (1844/3).
Owners. *2.2.1848:* Sold by High Court of Admiralty to Brian Coates, Rotherhithe. *7.2.1848:* Joseph Logan Thompson (s.o.), South Shields, acquired 48/64ths. *5.9.1850:* Enoch Donkerly Thompson (s.o.), South Shields, acquired 1/64ths from Joseph Logan Thompson. *16.12.1852:* Coates transferred his remaining 16/64ths to John Snowdon (s.o.), South Shields. *23.2.1853:* Henry & Thomas Henderson (22/64 & 21/64ths respectively) of Warkworth and Jane Elizabeth Henderson (21/64), North Shields.
Master. 17.3.1853: John Bell.

On 24 November 1855 the *Victoria* was sold to John Sidgwick, George & William Mears of Bishopwearmouth and Henry Longstaff, Sunderland. Her Custom House Register notes that she was "lost" on 2 March 1856.

162   *WARKWORTH* (1815-1833)
Snow   119 tons   67·5 x 20·5 feet
1815: Built Blyth by John Davison.
Owners. *2.6.1815:* Henry Muers (m.m.), Andrew Ramsey (m.t.) & John Muers (innkeeper), all Warkworth; Henry Taylor, Crofton. 26.10.1825 share distribution: Henry Muers (24/64), John Muers (32/64, innkeeper), both Warkworth; Executors of Henry Taylor (8/64).
Masters. *2.6.1815:* Henry Muers. *26.2.1821:* John Muers. *18.8.1825:* Henry Muers. *26.10.1825:* Henry Muers. 25.7.1829: Charles Dunn. 18.3.1831: William Brown.

The *Warkworth* was lost at Trouville, France, on 23 September 1833.

163   *WARKWORTH CASTLE* (1865-1881)   O/N 49786
Snow   269 tons   108·5 x 26·6 x 15·8 feet
1865: Built North Hylton, Sunderland, by L. Wheatley.
Owners. *8.9.1865:* James Shotton (32/64, s.o.,m.o.), Donald McInnis (10/64, grocer) & David Ditchburn (10/64, m.m.), all Amble; Robert Hardie (12/64, s.w.), Seelie(?), Fife. *19.1.1871:* Ditchburn & Hardie transferred their 22/64ths to Shotton. *19.8.1875:* Donald McInnis died; his 10/64ths transferred to Robert Green McInnis (grocer), Amble. *24.1.1877:* Shotton transferred 10/64ths to Edward Tuck (m.m.), Amble.

On 4 October 1880 the *Warkworth Castle* was reported to have been wrecked at Cimbutshama (possibly Simrishhamn, near Ystad) when on passage from Cronstadt to Gloucester with planks. However she was either salvaged or the report is erroneous for she became a total loss after going ashore at Garrucha during April 1881 when on passage from

Algiers to Carboneras. Her crew were saved. Edward Tuck, one of her share holders, was master.

164 *WAVE* (1855-1868)   O/N   15422
Schooner   162 tons   99·6 x 21·8 x 12·6 feet
1855: Built Blyth.
Owners. *18.10.1855:* Robert Simpson (32/64) & George Potter (32/64), both Alnmouth shipowners.

On 13 April 1868, the *Wave* was acquired by Edward Wilkinson of Blyth. In the following November he transferred 16/64ths and 10/16ths respectively to George & William Ealy, Blyth master mariners, and 12/64ths to James Wallace (teacher), of the same port.

In the November of 1876 the *Wave* (Capt. Davison) put into Copenhagen, leaky having struck a sunken rock. She was transferred to Rochester on 31 March 1881after being acquired by W.B. Frend

On 18 September 1887, the *Wave* foundered three miles west of Dungeness Light while on passage from South Shields towards Ouistrehan, France, with a cargo of coal and one passenger.

165 *WAVE SPIRIT* (1864-1868)   O/N 30373
ex *E.L. Walton.*
Brigantine (originally brig)   140 tons   90 x 24·5 x 9·9 feet
1846: Built Kennebunk, Maine.
P/R: Aberdeen (1863/2)
Owners. *10.8.1864:* John Duncan (26/64) & Alexander Young (6/64), both Amble; Alexander Potts (22/64, teacher) & Margaret Ann Potts (10/64, spinster), both Harbottle.

The *Wave Spirit* had formerly been the American coastal packet ship *E.L. Walton* running during 1848 with the Eagle Line from New York to Mobile, Alabama, and in the following year with the Hurlbuts Line.

As the Amble owned *Wave Spirit* she put into Shields Harbour on 3 December 1864 after encountering heavy weather on the Dogger Bank during a passage from Riga to London. A heavy sea had struck her carrying away bulwarks, rails, stanchions and covering boards.

She was lost after catching fire off Seaham on 23 November 1868.

166 *WEE TOTTIE* (1845-1848)
Snow   163 tons   78 x 21·2 x 12·9 feet
1845: Built Bill Quay by William Boutland.
Owner. *26.6.1845:* Thomas Browne, Amble.
Masters. *26.6.1845:* John Phillips. *26.7.1845:* Robert Buckham. *14.10.1845:* John Brown.

On 8 February 1848 the *Wee Tottie* was sold to Simon Samuel, a Llanlly (? Llanelli) master mariner, and transferred to that port ten days later.

167 *WIDDRINGTON* (1817-1835)
Snow   127 tons   66·2 x 21·3 x 11·9 feet
1815: Built Sunderland by David Watt.
Owners: *4.11.1815:* John Stafford (coal fitter), Monkwearmouth. *25.3.1817:* Joseph Hardy, Alnwick.
Master. *25.3.1833*: Charles Reed.

On 14 November 1833 the *Widdrington's* registration was cancelled and endorsed: "in consequence of vessel having received an excess of foreign repairs by which the British

The *Widdrington* under all plain sail.

privileges of said ship are forfeited." However there must have been a change of mind for on 9 January 1835 she was sold to Ralph Grey (21/64, s.o.), Charles Reed (21/64) & William Swan (22/64, butcher), all Newcastle. They had her until 18 April 1836 when Charles Reed, William & George Carr of Berwick became the owners and had her transferred to their home town.

During 1872 the *Widdrington* (Capt. R. Coulson) spent nearly six weeks in Amble. She had arrived with a cargo of pit props from Gothenburg and left with coal for Boulogne.

In Sir Walter Runciman's *Collier Brigs and their Sailors*, it is noted that she was sunk in collision in the Yarmouth Roads on 9 December 1872. He remarks that the *Widdrington* was: "One of the oldest coasters; very popular with sailors."

168 **WIDGEON** (1879-1889)   O/N 45600
Snow   229 tons   101·3 x 26 x 15·1 feet.
Capacity: 18 keels
1863: Built Sunderland by Gray & Young.
Owners. *23.3.1863:* John William Popplewell (s.o.), Preston, North Shields. *31.2.1863:* Reed Stonebank (m.m.), North Shields, acquired 8/64ths. *13.2.1867:* Joseph Hodgson (s.b.), Blyth. *15.4.1867:* James Turnbull (s.br.), Blyth. *15.3.1879:* Hugh Andrews (coal owner, Broomhill Coal Co.), Amble.

When hailing from Blyth and Amble, the *Widgeon* featured in the *Casualty Lists* on a number of occasions:

14.4.1877: Malmo to Riga in ballast. Ashore near Arensburg, Island of Oesel, during snow storm.

27.1.1880: Amble to Calais. Run down by steam trawler *Stephensons* near Coquet Is and. Stern cut right through, port side of deck hove-up. Towed into Tyne by trawler.

14.11.1882: Chatham Dockyard to Amble in ballast. Went ashore at Pakefield after parting from anchors. Lifeboat unable to help due to heavy sea - three men and coxswain washed overboard. Widgeon's crew of nine saved by the Lowestoft Rocket Apparatus.

87

When sold in 1879 for £700, by her Blyth owner to Hugh Andrews it was noted that the *Widgeon:* "had cost late owner upwards of £2,000 a few years ago" (*Newcastle Daily Journal, 7 April 1879*). As an Amble ship she was commanded by William Porter for much of the time. Here are some examples of her wanderings with him as master:

1879 Amble to Elsinore   7 days
        Amble to Travemunde   12 days
1880 Algiers to Falmouth.
1882 Amble (sailed 18 January) to Calais
        Amble (sailed 27 June) to Stockholm
        Stockholm to Hudiksvall (arrived 23 July).

On 13 July 1889 the *Widgeon* was acquired by George Hall, a North Shields mariner. This transaction was followed by a number of share changes - *22.8.1889:* John Elliott (ship chandler), Howdon, acquired 32/64ths. *30.9.1889:* Elliott transferred 16/64ths to William Milburn (ships husband), North Shields. *25.4.1890:* Milburn returned his 16/64ths to Elliott. *16.3.1891:* Elliott transferred his 32/64ths to Edward McCormack & Alfred Nicholls, both Newcastle shipowners. *18.11.1895:* George Hall again became sole owner.

The *Widgeon's* register was closed on 28 December 1910; she had been broken up at Sunderland the previous year.

169   **WILD ROSE** (1863-1880)   O/N 45626
Snow   252 tons   102·2 x 25·9 x 15·7 feet
9.12.1863: Launched at Sunderland from yard of B.& J. Gardner.
Owners. *22.12.1863:* John Henry Barry (50/64, s.o.) & John Claxton jun., (3/64, m.m.), both Amble; John Barry (8/64, s.o.) & John Claxton (3/64, m.m.), both Whitby. *28.12.1863:* John Claxton jun., transferred his 3/64ths to John Claxton, Whitby. *29.8.1868:* John Claxton, Whitby, died; John Claxton jun, Amble, inherited his 6/64ths.

The brig *Wild Rose* lying at Porthmadoc in 1889 when Welsh owned.
(By permission of Gwynedd Archives Service)

The *Wild Rose* was the second vessel to be built by B.& J. Gardner for John Henry Barry. Intended for the Baltic and Mediterranean trades, she was fitted with Cunningham's patent reefing topsail. Capt. John Claxton jun., transferred from Barry's *Eliza & Jane* to take command. On 1 June 1868, at eleven o'clock at night, the *Wild Rose* was beating down Channel under all plain sail, except royals. There was a light fog lying. At twenty minutes past the hour a fog horn was heard on the port bow, then, almost immediately a barque was seen running before the wind. She struck the *Wild Rose's* port bow carrying away bowsprit, figure head and cutwater. The foremast went by the board along with some stanchions and rails. The barque proved to be the *J.L.Thiedman* (Philadelphia to Bremen). She stood by the *Wild Rose* until midnight then went on her way. It was not until three o'clock the following afternoon that the tug *Dreadnaught* came along, put a line on board, and got her into Dover Harbour.

In 1869 a 45 day passage was made from New York to Queenstown (Cobh) and in 1877 it took her 51 days to come from Cronstadt to the Tyne. She arrived on 10 November with boats stove and cargo shifted.

The *Wild Rose's* register was closed following her sale to Norwegian owners on 14 May 1880. *Lloyd's Register* for 1887 lists her as being owned by Johs. Torresen, of Mandal. Beside the entry the ominous word "wrecked" has been stamped but that was by no means the end of the *Wild Rose*. She had certainly been driven ashore at Afon Wen, near Criccieth, and was in such a bad way as to earn the title "wreck." However, she was later re-floated, re-fitted and returned to the British flag, and, in July, 1887, acquired by Samuel Prydderch Owen, a contractor of Porthmadog. He sent her out to Pensacola for a cargo of timber for her new home port. But Owen was not destined to have the *Wild Wave* for long. He died on 17 October 1887 and his executors sold her to William Jones, a sailmaker, also of Porthmadog. She was eventually lost off Para, on the coast of Brazil, on 19 June 1889.

170   *WILLIAM* (1871-1878)   O/N 10107
Barque   370 tons   117·4 x 27·6 x 17·1 feet
1857: Built Sunderland by R. Candlish.
Owners. *2.3.1857:* William Christopher Allen (22/64) & John Allen (21/64), both South Shields shipowners; Robert Scott Briggs (12/64) & Charles James Briggs (9/64), both Sunderland ship brokers. *22.9.1859:* William Christopher Allen (33/64), Robert Scott Briggs (12/64), Charles James Briggs (9/64) & John Morrison (10/64, s.o.), South Shields. *7.1.1869:* Edward & Joseph Lumsden (32/64ths each, chain & anchor manufacturers), both Sunderland. *26.2.1869:* William Patterson & William Rogerson (32/64ths each), both Newcastle. *8.4.1871*: James Calder (22/64), David Ditchburn (21/64) & Robert Hardie (21/64), all Amble shipowners. *5.4.1873:* Hardie transferred his 21/64ths to Edward Alder (s.o.), Amble. *29.3.1874:* Edward Alder died. *27.3.1876:* Alder's 21/64ths transferred to James Calder. *28.4.1876:* James Calder became sole owner.

On 27 January 1873 the *William* was found derelict, with 13 feet of water in her hold, eleven miles south-south-west of the Eddystone Light by the pilot cutter *Ferret* whose crew managed to beach her at Cattewater, near Plymouth. Bound to Cadiz, she had been abandoned, leaking badly, the previous day during bad weather. Her crew had been taken off by the Tyne barque *Affiance* and landed at Falmouth. During March 1878 the *William* was sold at Harwich to be broken up or used as a coal hulk.

171   *ZEALOUS* (1853-1861)   O/N 26268
Brig   129 tons   67·8 x 19 x 12·9 feet
1827: Built Limekilns, Fife.
P/R: London (1852/67).

Owners. *28.6.1853:* Sold by Thomas Forsyth Watson, Shadwell, & William Watson jun., Rotherhith, to George Hall (m.m.), Amble.
Masters. *12.7.1853:* George Hall. *23.2.1854:* Robert Alder. *8.4.1854* George Hall. *27.3.1855:* Robert Dawson.

On 2 November 1861, when bound from Amble towards Boulogne, a sea broke aboard and knocked the *Zealous's* stern frame in. Rendered unmanageable, her crew took to the long boat and were picked up by the *Ariel* of Seaham. The *Zealous* foundered off the Yorkshire Coast the following day.

172   **ZETUS** (1868)   O/N 28587
Barque   300 tons   110·1 x 26·1 x 16·5 feet
1860: Built Sunderland by Pace & Blumer.
Owners. *4.10.1860:* William Milburn (27/64) & Edmund Hannay Watts jun. (16/64), both Blyth ship brokers; Arthur Cox Pring (21/64, m.t.), Newcastle. *11.5.1868:* John Punshon Denton, a Hartlepool ship builder. *4.6.1868:* John Turnbull (s.o.), Amble.

After only five months as an Amble ship, the *Zetus* (Capt. Turnbull) was wrecked off Malta.

Owners
&
Shareholders

As a seaport, with roots going back six centuries or more, Alnmouth understandably had an established group of shipowners well before the period of this study which commences in the 1830's. The Gibbs family were prominent and, amongst others, the corn merchants Thomas Annett, John Appleby and John Wilkinson had considerable shipping interests in the 1820's. Over the years, Robert Simpson, who acted as ships' agent and wharfinger, possessed shares in ten of the smaller sailing ships. Further upstream, at Alnwick, George Simpson and various members of the Davison family participated in the ownership and management of the world ranging barques *Aydon Forest, Campsie Glen, Manfred, Oliver* and the London registered *Kentish Tar*. All fine ships, specially built for their Alnwick owners, they averaged around about the 500 registered ton mark.

As Amble grew as a sea port, it bred its own community of shipowners. Some of the ships were the property of one person, notably Thomas Browne and Hugh Andrews who were the sole owners of considerable fleets, others belonged to particular families but, for the most part, they were owned by groups of people who joined together to buy shares in an individual ship. These were sometimes referred to as sixty-fourthers, a name brought about by the 1824 Ship Registration Act which began the practice of dividing the ownership of a ship into sixty-four shares. Most shares were held in multiples of four. Sixteen sixty-fouths (16/64ths) being a common holding. At the end of a trading period, the profit and losses were divided up according to the number of shares held.

Many of share-holders described themselves as shipowners without ever owning a ship outright, preferring to spread their investments in a number of vessels. One or two of them would be regarded as the owner(s) for management purposes.

While most of the shareholders had connections with the shipping industry such as shipbuilders, master mariners and the like, there were a great many other professions and trades represented. Amongst the shareholders of the barque *Kedron* were a cordwainer, an agriculturalist and a medical student. The *Meggie Dixon* had the deputy-coronor of Morpeth amongst its shareholders and the Alnmouth schooner *Adventure* a King's Messenger! Women in those days were described as either spinsters or widows in the shipping registers, there was never a missus amongst them. Once married, any shares they might have held became the property of their husbands.

It is not pretended that the following list is complete in respect of either owners or the ships they owned. Some owners, as they prospered moved to Newcastle where they opened offices near the centres of commercial activity. Hugh Andrews, the proprietor of Warkworth Harbour, coal, and ship owner had offices in Queen Street, Newcastle. In such circumstances their ships, in time, may well have been considered as Tyne owned. Just occasionally an owner would have a ship registered at a port well outside the area. This was sometimes inherited when second hand tonnage was bought. Hugh Andrew's brigantine *Stork* was registered in London. The author served for nearly five years aboard ships belonging to the ancestors of a personality mentioned in this account. Their place of business was in Newcastle, the ships were managed from there, most of the officers were North-East men, indeed to everyone concerned with the shipping industry they were Newcastle ships. Yet both were registered in London, a name which was painted very distinctly on their sterns.

Abrahamsen S. (Brevig) 21
Adams, John (s.b.; Newcastle) 82
Adams, Lancelot (glass m.f.; Hartley) 82
Adamson & Co. (London) 128
Adamson, Henry E.P. (s.o.; Newcastle) 68
Addison, Wm. (tallow chandler; Newcastle) 11
Adler, Edward (m.m.; Amble) 129
Aikonow, Alex. (s.br.; London) 78
Alder, Edward (s.o.; Amble
[*died 29.3.1874*]) 170
Allan, Walter (iron m.t.; Tynemouth) 115
Allen, Jas. (draper; Alnwick) 78
Allen, John (s.o.; S.Shields) 170
Allen, Thos. (m.t.; Newcastle) 11
Allen, Wm. C. (s.o.; S.Shields) 170
Allison, Mary A. (widow; Sunderland) 90
Anderson, John (ship repairer; Felling) 129
Andrews, Hugh (coal, colliery & ship owner; Amble, Eastfield Hall, Felton [Park], Newcastle, Swarland & Warkworth Harb. [*died 27.5.1926*]) 11, 18, 22, 32, 36, 42, 49, 68, 75, 95, 109, 113, 143, 144, 157, 158, 160, 168

Appleby, John (corn factor, corn m.t.; Buston, Low Buston [*died c1840*]) 7, 8, 46, 51, 105
Apsen, Wm. (Rotherhithe) 91
Armstrong, John (carpenter; Newcastle) 59
Armstrong, Thos. (m.m.; Blyth) 113
Armstrong, Thos. (carpenter; Newcastle) 59
Arnett, John W. (farmer; Wigham) 14
Atkinson, Elizabeth (widow; Alnmouth) 112
Atkinson, Matt. H. (s.o.; N.Shields) 131
Austin, Samuel P. (s.b.; Sunderland) 29, 43, 155
Ayre, Jas. (s.o.; Sunderland) 103, 115
Bailes, Matt. (ship keeper; Sunderland) 106
Bain, Robt. (m.m.; Alnmouth) 127
Bainbridge, Jas. (Durham) 39, 139
Barker, Chris D. (banker; Worcester) 49
Barker, Thos. (s.o.; S.Shields) 49
Barry & Co. (Whitby) 20, 98
Barry J.H. (Whitby) 96
Barry, John (s.o.; Whitby) 117, 138, 169,
Barry, John H. (s.o.; Amble) 23, 24, 80, 131, 169

Hugh Andrews came to the area from Belfast in about 1869. In time he became owner of the Radcliffe and Broomhill Collieries as well as Warkworth Harbour. He began shipowning in 1871 with the building of the steamer *Warkworth* on the Tyne.. His first sailing ship was the brigantine *Union T* , purchased three years later. Most of his sailing ships were managed by John Park. In 1900 he sold out to Sir Christopher Furness but retained an interest in the companies which were subsequently formed to run the collieries, harbour and ships. He appears to have spent the rest of his life in the south country. His address in the 1912 edition of the *Mercantile Navy List and Maritime Directory* is given as Toddingham Manor, Winchcombe, Gloucestershire. He was then owner of the steam yacht *Taurus*. See also *Appendix II* and *General Index*.

Anholm W.B.S. (Aberdeen) 81
Annett, John W. (farmer; Ulgham) 100
Annett, Thos. (corn m.t.; Alnmouth
[*died c1830*]) 46, 102, 112

Baxter, David (Whitby) 120
Bedlington, Isaac (West Hartlepool) 64
Bell, John (marine store dealer; S.Shields) 152

Bell, Robt. (s.w.; Blyth) 4
Bird, Geo. (S.Shields) 134
Bisson, Wm. (Jersey) 132
Blythe & Greene (London) 111
Booker, Josias (Allerton) 92
Boutland, John G. (s.o.; Bill Quay) 155
Boutland, Wm. (s.b.; Bill Quay) 120
Boutland, Wm. E. (s.b.; Bill Quay) 155

Brown, Thos. (labourer; Sheriff Hill) 141
Brown, Wm. (labourer; West Hartlepool) 141
Brown, Wm.J. (Seaham) 155
Browne, Elizabeth (spinster; Amble House, Warkworth) 26
Browne, Thos. (coal owner, s.o.; Amble, Amble House) 10, 26, 27, 39, 47, 48, 83, 91, 120, 139, 140, 153, 166

A London based solicitor, Thomas Browne came to Amble in about 1835 as co-lessee of the Radcliffe Colliery. His shipowning activities began in 1838 with the purchase of the schooner *Lady Nepean*. By 1844 his financial position was becoming "suspect" as evidenced by the case of the 235 ton brig *George*. During November 1844 he entered into an agreement with George Gray for the construction of this vessel at Friar's Goose, near Gateshead, at a cost of £2,050. She was completed about eight months later. Browne then offered Gray half the purchase money and the remainder in Bills of Exchange. This arrangement was unacceptable to Gray who promptly had the brig registered in his own name as the *George* and sent her on a voyage to Marseilles. Browne became bankrupt in 1848 and his ships were sold. The *Newcastle Journal* of 28 October 1848 advertises for sale by auction at the home of Martin Henderson, Wellwood Arms Inn, Amble, a 4/64th interest in an "excellent steam vessel called the *Ellen Browne*" by the "Assignees of Thomas Browne, bankrupt." The *Ellen Browne* was a tug. She was still going strong well into the 1860's.

Bowman & Drummond (shipbuilders; Blyth) 31
Brandt H.T. (Copenhagen) 40
Branfoot, Wm. (s.o.; Sunderland) 154, 155
Brenan, John H. (London) 37
Briggs, Chas.J. (s.br.; Sunderland) 170
Briggs, Robt. S. (s.br.; Sunderland) 170
Brock, Thos. (timber m.t.; Glasgow) 128
Brooks, Elijah (forgeman; Newcastle) 143
Broomhill Coal Co. (Amble) 144, 168
Brown, Chas. (Dunbar) 156
Brown, Geo. (m.m.; Blyth) 141
Brown, Jas. (m.m.; London) 5
Brown, Jonathan (Gateshead) 102
Brown, Jos. (s.b.; Liverpool) 37
Brown, Jos. (Middlesborough) 115
Brown, Mary (widow; Forrest Hall) 81
Brown, Mary (Morpeth) 108
Brown, Robert E. (deputy-coroner; Morpeth) 108
Brown, Thos. (m.t., builder; Warkworth) 81, 85
Brown, Thos. (s.o.; Newcastle) 89
Brown, Thos. (m.m.; Clay) 122

Bruce, John (tobacconist; Alnwick) 100
Burchard A. (Rostock) 86
Burdon, Wm. (s.o.; Monkwearmouth) 113
Burgon, Jas. (fisherman; Eyemouth) 52
Burn, Geo. (m.m.; Amble) 152
Burn, Ralph (s.w.; Blyth) 143
Burnett, Chas. (m.m.) 139
Burnman, Charlotte (widow; N.Shields) 158
Bushell, John B. (s.b.; S.Shields) 40
Cairns, Geo. J. (farmer; Alnwick) 100
Cairns, John R.T. (farmer; Alnwick) 100
Calder, Jas. (contractor; Warkworth) 3
Calder, Jas. (s.o.; Amble) 54, 170
Candlish, Henry (Alnwick) 100
Candlish, John (s.o.; Sunderland) 25
Carr, Geo. (Berwick) 167
Carr, Wm. (Berwick) 167
Chalmers, Lewis (Aberdeen) 62
Chambers, Andrew (Amble) 155
Chambers, Wm. (pilot; Blyth) 143
Channel Coaling Co. 11
Chargeurs Reunis (France) 108
Chatwood, John (druggist; London) 107
Chisholm, Francis (m.m.; Amble) 129

Foster, Francis (m.t.; Alnmouth) 53
Foster, Geo. (s.o.; Monkwearmouth) 41
Foster, John (agent; Newcastle) 153
Foster, John R. (Blyth) 75
Foster, Wm. (m.m.; N.Shields) 152
Fountains Northumberland Trust (Amble) 116
Frederick, John (m.m.; Monkwearmouth) 48
Frend W.B. (Rochester) 164.
Friers, Michael S. (tobacconist; Alnwick) 14, 100
Gair, Wm. (m.m.; Amble) 61
Gallon, Matthew (S.Shields & London) 112
Gallon, Wm. (S.Shields) 112
Gann, Geo. H. (s.o.; Whitstable) 74, 78
Gann, Henry (s.o.; Whitstable) 74, 78
Gardner, Jas. (s.b.; Sunderland) 14
Garrow, Jas. (Montrose) 38
Garth, Geo. (Monkwearmouth) 106
Gatley, Clarinda L. (spinster; St Marys, Cornwall) 89
Gatley, Claringa L. (Alnwick) 14
Gatley, Louisa C. (spinster; St Marys, Cornwall) 89
Gibb, Edward (m.m.; Alnmouth & Amble) 17, 46, 71, 102, 107, 112, 146
Gibb, Geo. (m.m.; Alnmouth & Warkworth [*died c1825*]) 46, 102, 156
Gibb, Henry (m.m.; Alnmouth) 45
Gibb, Henry G. (m.m.; Alnmouth) 2, 99, 121, 127
Gibb, Isabella (widow; Alnmouth) 145
Gibb, John H. (m.m.; Amble & Alnmouth) 30, 61, 76
Gibb, Robt. (m.m.; Alnmouth) 46, 76
Gibbon, Arthur (Acklington Park) 149
Gibbon, Robt. (Warkworth Cottage) 149
Gibbs, Wm. (Rotherhithe) 91
Gibson, Geo. (Cowpen) 75
Gibson, Hannah (widow; S.Shields) 41
Gibson, John (s.o., m.m.; Blyth) 126, 156
Gilmore, John (ship broker & valuer, Liverpool) 115.5
Gilray, Robt. (engineer; Tynemouth) 82
Glaholm, Thos. (rope maker; Sunderland) 159
Glass, John (school master; Amble) 61
Gloriana Sailing Ship Co. (Dublin) 54
Glover, John (s.br.; London) 103
Graden, Thos. (provision m.t.; Newcastle) 54

Graham J. & Sons, 115·5
Gray W.S. (Gateshead) 96
Gray, Henry (N.Sunderland) 125
Gray, Martin F. (harb., master; Amble) 61
Gray, Wm. (fish m.t.; Amble) 66
Green, Robt. (agent & s.o.; Togston & Warkworth) 3, 92, 117, 138
Green, Thos. (confectioner; N.Shields) 108
Greenwell, Robt. (Bishopwearmouth) 1
Grey, Ralph (s.o.; Newcastle) 167
Grey, Robt.,T. (banker; Alnwick) 100
Grey, Wm. J. (s.b.; Newcastle) 151
Griffith, David (Rotherhithe) 91
Hale, L. (Broadstairs) 51
Haley A. (Sydney, C.B.) 18
Hall, Geo. (s.o.; Amble) 129, 142, 171
Hall, Geo. (mariner; N. Shields) 168
Halliday, Richard H. (m.m., Sunderland) 146
Hardie, Robt. (m.m., s.o., s.w.; Amble & Seelie[?]) 3, 163, 170
Hardy, Jas. (m.t.; Alnwick) 134
Hardy, Jos. (Alnwick) 167
Harper J. (London) 140
Harrison, Andrew (Sunderland) 103
Harrison, Jas. (s.w.; Amble) 54
Harrison, John (m.t. & s.w.; Amble & Radcliffe Colliery) 33, 54
Harrison, John G. (S.Shields) 11
Harrison, Jos. (s.o., Radcliffe & Warkorth) 37, 146
Harrison, Jos. (m.t.; Newcastle) 33
Harrison, Wm.S. (Sunderland) 103
Hart, John (S.Shields) 112
Haswell, John (s.b.; Sunderland) 103
Hawks, Geo. (iron m.t.; London) 102
Hawks, John (iron m.t.; Gateshead) 102
Hawks, Robert S. (iron m.t.; Gateshead) 102
Hay, Wm. (m.t.; Bishopwearmouth) 115
Hay, Wm. C. (Amble) 64
Heatley, Henry (draper, m.m., s.o.; Alnmouth & Alnwick) 45, 76, 79, 145
Heatley, Jas. (m.m., s.o.; Blyth) 29, 72, 159
Heatley, Jas. (agent; Amble) 73
Heatley, Jeff. (draper; Alnmouth) 76
Hedley, Jas. (m.t.; Newcastle) 82
Hedley, Robt. (m.m.; Amble) 78, 103
Henderson, Elizabeth (widow; Amble) 40
Henderson, Francis (N.Shields) 108
Henderson, Gilbert (m.m., s.o.; Newcastle) 37, 120

Henderson, Henry (m.t., postmaster, s.o.; Warkworth) 63, 69, 115, 161
Henderson, Issac (m.m.; Sunderland) 134
Henderson, Jane E. (spinster, N.Shields) 63, 69, 115, 161
Henderson, Jas. (m.m.; Amble) 52
Henderson, John (gas m.f., m.t., s.o., Amble & Hauxley [*died 20.1.1874*]) 15, 30, 37, 40, 45, 52, 97, 146
Henderson, John (plumber; Amble [*died 5.3.1867*]) 65
Henderson, John (farmer; Widrington) 110
Hendersonn, John J. (m.t.; N.Shields) 69
Henderson, John M. (m.o., s.o.; Amble) 5, 13, 43, 111, 128
Henderson, Thos. (m.t., s.o.; Warkworth) 63, 69, 115, 161
Henderson, Thos. H. (Newcastle) 79
Henoch J.G.C. (Bremen) 86
Herdsman, John (medical doctor; Lesbury) 31
Heron, Jas. (s.o.; Blyth) 132
Heslop, Wm. (innkeeper; Newcastle) 132
Hewson, Shallet (s.o.; North Shields [*died 12.6.71*]) 5
Hine W. & Co. 44
Hindmarch, Henry (blacksmith; Alnmouth) 2, 17, 127
Hindmarch, Luke (m.t., s.o.; Alnmouth & Alnwick) 16, 44, 84, 87
Hindmarch, Wm. (m.t.; Alnwick) 16, 84
Hodgeson, Jos. (Crofton Mill) 51
Hodgson, John (Crofton Mill) 106
Hodgson, Joseph (s.b., s.o.; Crofton & Blyth) 8, 106, 168
Holdsworth, John F. (farmer, s.o.; Amble) 23, 24, 80
Hopper, Thos. (Stockton) 127
Horritt, Adam (cordwainer;Warkworth) 85
Horritt, Geo. (cordwainer; Warkworth) 85
Horritt, Robt. (cordwainer; Warkworth) 85
Horritt, Thos. S. (m.m.; Warkworth) 85
Horsley, Jas. (m.t.; Alnwick) 100
Horsley, John J. (m.t.; Alnwick) 100
Howitt, Thos S. (m.m., s.o.; Amble, Dunoon, Reading & Warkworth) 67, 81, 89, 108
Hubbard, John (hoop m.t.; London) 103
Hudson, Geo. (s.o.; Monkwearmouth) 16
Hudson, Geo. W. (s.o.; Sunderland) 25

Hudson, Jane (widow; Felton) 80
Hudson, Margaret (spinster; Felton) 80
Hudson, Ralph M. (s.o.; Sunderland) 25
Hunter, John (Bishopwearmouth) 1
Hunter, John Wm. (Sunderland) 1
Huntress, John (m.m.; S.Shields) 148
Hurlbuts Line (U.S.A.) 165
Hurry, Francis (N.Shields) 11
Hurry, Francis (s.b.; Howdon) 11
Hurry, Thos. (s.b.; Howdon) 11
Hurry, Thos. (N.Shields) 11
Hurst, Luke (agent; Liverpool) 123
Hutchinson Geo. C. (s.b.; Newcastle) 61
Hutchinson, Ralph (s.o.; Bishopwearmouth) 115
Ingo, John (s.o.; Newcastle) 82
Jack, Richard (manager; Newcastle) 157
Jackson, John R. (m.m.; Amble) 74
James, Benj. (s.o., Yarmouth) 90
Jameson, Thos. (m.m.; Newcastle) 82
Jefferson, Thos. (W.Hartlepool) 146
Johnson A. (Stavanger) 3
Johnson, Geo. G. (m.m.; S.Shields) 41
Johnson, Wm. (grocer; Fawdon) 150
Jolly, Robt. (m.t.; S.Shields) 84
Jones, Wm. (sailmaker, Porthmadog) 169
Jopling, Edward (Sunderland) 141
Judson, Geo. (m.m., s.o.; Seaham Harbour) 92, 138
June, Wm. (timber m.t., Hartlepool) 115·5.
Kelso, John Robt. (N.Shields) 134
Kent, Albert (Mevagissey) 117
Kent, John (Mevagissey) 117
Kirkley, Ann (widow; N.Shields) 11
Kirkwood, Wm. (s.o.; Monkwearmouth) 16
Knott, Jas. (s.o.; Newcastle) 35
Laing, Chas. (s.o.; N.Shields) 11
Laing, John (s.o.; N.Shields) 11
Laing, Robt. (St Leonards) 43
Lamb, Thos. (innkeeper; Amble) 61
Lange, Carl (m.t.; Newcastle) 33
Larsen S.C. (Brevig) 21
Lawes, John W. (S.Shields) 36
Lawn, Robt. (s.o., Hartlepool) 109.
Leaker, Thos. H. (Bristol) 150
Leaker, Wm. R.H. (Bristol) 150
Leask, Jos.& Co. (Lerwick) 11
Lee, Geo. (s.b.; Tweedmouth) 34
Lee, John (butcher; Newcastle) 35

Leighton, Thos. (grocer, s.b., s.o.; Amble) 1, 3, 9, 30, 61, 62, 123, 129
Leighton, Wm. (m.m.; Liverpool) 123
Lilburn, Geo. (King's messenger; London) 2
Linskill, Wm. (N.Shields) 11
Lisle, Wm. (Seaham Harbour) 41
Little, Geo. (m.t.; Monkwearmouth) 82
Longstaff, Henry (Sunderland) 161
Lorho J. (Vannes) 108
Lumsden, Edward (chain & anchor m.f.; Sunderland) 170
Lumsden, Jos. (chain & anchor m.f.; Sunderland) 170
Mackenzie, Donald (Stornoway) 90
Mackenzie, John (Blyth) 1
Malcamson, Wm. (s.o.; Sunderland) 1
Mann, Crane (N.Shields) 108
Mann, Isaac C. (m.m., s.o.; Amble, N. Shields & Warkworth) 58, 60, 108
Mann, Robt. (Clay [died c1852]) 93
Marchbank, Wm. G. (s.b.; Newcastle) 151
Marshall, Frank (rope maker; S. Blyth) 148
Marshall, Geo. (s.o.; Killingworth) 67
Marshall, Geo. (labourer; N. Shields) 85
Marshall, Geo. (clerk; Newcastle) 89
Marshall, John (s.o.; Amble) 88
Marshall, Wm. (agriculturist; Lesbury) 85
Martin, John (s.o.; N. Shields) 55
Mason, Geo. (m.t.; Amble [died 25.9.68])13
Mather, Robt. (Amble) 155
Matthews, Robt. (pilot; Amble) 74
Matthews, Wm. (Cullercoats) 41
Mattison, John (m.m.; Alnmouth) 107
May, John (m.m.; Aberdeen) 100
McBrayne, Duncan (s.o.; Sunderland) 60
McCauler, Henry (m.m.; N.Shields) 14
McCormack, Edward (Newcastle) 168
McDonald, Jas. (St Margarets Hope) 108
McDougal, Wm. (Alnwick) 130
McInnes, Donald (grocer; Warkworth) 92, 117, 163
McInnes, Donald (m.t.; Amble [died 19.4.1875]) 3
McInnes, Donald (grocer; Amble [died 19.8.1875]) 163
McInnes, R. G. & Co. (Amble) 94

McInnes, Robt. G. (grocer; Amble) 163
Mackenle Y, David (builder, s.o.; Alnwick) 19, 50, 67, 86, 101, 108, 114, 122
McKenzie, David (Alnwick) 136
McQuillen, Henry (Lesbury) 100
Mears, Geo. (Bishopwearmouth) 161
Mears, William (Bishopwearmouth) 161
Mekkelsen P. (Brevig) 21
Melrose Wm. E. (s.o.; Amble) 25
Melrose, Isabella (widow; Amble) 56
Melrose, Wm. E. (s.o.; Amble [died ⁻23.5.1878]) 56, 74
Meyden, D. van de Harlingen 118
Middlemass, Robt. (?) 108
Miekle Wm. (rope m.f.; Newcastle) 61
Milburn, Wm. (m.o., s,o, s.br., ships husband; Blyth, Newcastle & N. Shields) 35, 57, 58, 60, 137, 168, 172
Milhush & Co. (London) 30
Miller & Co. (Liverpool) 36
Miller, Edward (mariner; Beer, Devon) 62
Miller, Jas. (colliery agent; Newcastle) 35
Miller, Jos. (butcher; Southwick) 138
Mirio J. (Bordeaux) 24
Moffat, David (draper; Newcastle) 61
Moncur, Isabella (spirit dealer; Dundee) 102
Moone, David (N. Sunderland) 59
Moorson, Peter (m.m.; Robin Hood's Bay) 35
Morrison, Edward (steam boat owner; Blyth) 143
Morrison, John (s.o.; S.Shields) 170
Muers, Henry (m.m.; Warkworth) 162
Muers, John (innkeeper; Warkworth) 162
Muras, John (m.m.; Amble) 92, 110
Murdock, John (Bishopwearmouth) 140
Murray, Ann (N.Shields) 108
Nairn, Jas. (stonemason; Amble) 123
Nelson, Henry (Starcross) 124
Nicholls, Alfred (Newcastle) 168
Nicholson, Alex. (broker; London) 103
Nicholson, Geo. (m.m.; Blyth) 143
Nielson C. (Laurvig [?Larvik]) 21
Osbourn, Jas. (m.m.; S.Shields) 152
Oxley, Stephen (m.m.; Seaton Sluice [died 5.10.1845]) 134

Robert Green McInnes survived to become, at the age of 84, Amble's oldest native. That was in 1930. He was born and lived in a house in Church Street all his life. Very active in public affairs, he was a member of the Harbour Commission.

Simpson, Robt. (ship agent, s.o., wharf-inger; Alnmouth) 6, 31, 46, 72, 73, 99, 121, 127, 159, 164

Simpson, Robt. (commercial traveller; London) 29

Simpson, Thos. (victualler; Alnmouth) 71

Sinclair, Jas. (commission agent; Berwick) 70

Sinclair, Samuel (rope maker; Sunderland) 159

Singleton (Glasgow) 40

Skelly, John (farmer; Denwick [died c1846]) 59, 70, 125

Smith J.T. (London) 26

Smith, Aaron (Alnwick) 148

Smith, Adam (Alemouth) 34

Smith, Duncan (m.m.; Alnwick) 19

Smith, E.P. (London) 32

Smith, Geo. (Fogston) 104

Smith, Jas. (m.m.; Liverpool) 1

Smith, Jas. (s.o.; Sunderland) 1

Smith, Jas. (m.m., s.o.; Amble) 9, 12, 123, 133

Smith, Jas. (Montrose) 38

Smith, Jas. (Rotherhithe) 91

Smith, Ralph (m.t.; Alnmouth & Alnwick) 130, 149

Smith, Robt. (m.m.; Monkwearmouth) 104

Smith, Thompson (s.b.; Willington) 150

Smith, Thos. (s.b.; Newcastle) 87

Smith, Thos.G. (coal owner; Fogston) 151

Smith, Wm. (m.m.; Amble) 1

Smith, Wm. (s.b.; Newcastle) 87

Snowball, Wm. (Sunderland) 154

Snowdon, John (s.o.; S.Shields) 161

Snowdon, Richard (Louth) 112

Spence, Andrew (Broughton Ferry) 153

Spittle, Henry (baker; Alnwick) 14, 19

Spittle, Wm. D. (m.t.; Alnwick) 100

Stafford, Bolton (Blyth) 106

Stafford, Francis (s.o.; Blyth) 143

Stafford, John (coal fitter; Monkwearmouth) 167

Stainton, Thos. (iron founder; S.Shields) 115

Stamp, Richard (farmer; Widrington) 110

Stanley, Wm. (iron m.t.; London) 102

Stanton, Geo. J. (s.o.; Alnmouth [died 20.4.1877]) 35, 119

Stanton, Wm. (s.o.; Alnmouth [died 7.6.1870]) 35

Stephenson, Dixon (butcher; Sunderland) 117, 142

Stephenson, Henry D. (Sunderland) 41

Stephenson, Wm. (s.o.; Alnmouth) 35

Stewart, John (m.m.; Newcastle) 125

Stonebank, Reed (m.m.; N.Shields) 168

Storm, Matthew (Whitby) 120

Straker, Geo. (Gateshead) 156

Straker, Jas. (s.o.; N.Shields) 134

Straughan, Wm. (builder; Alnmouth) 100

Surtees, Geo. (s.o.; Monkwearmouth) 16

Surtees, Geo. (s.b., s.o.; Amble & Wark-worth) 16, 38

Surtees, Wm. (m.m., s.o.; Monkwearmouth) 4, 16

Swan, Wm. (butcher; Newcastle) 167

Taylor, Ann (Seaton Sluice) 134

Taylor, Ellen A. (Alnwick) 108

Taylor, Henry (Sunderland) 64

Taylor, Henry (Crofton) 162

Taylor, Philip (Seaton Sluice) 134

Taylor, Robt. (coal m.t.; Dundee) 36

Temple, John (m.m.; Warkworth [died 30.12.1860]) 141

Temple, Mary A. (widow; Warkworth) 141

Thew, Conrad (m.t.; Alnwick) 31

Thew, Ed ward (m.t., s.o.; Alnwick & Lesbury Mills) 6, 8, 46, 51, 99, 106, 130, 149

Thiedeman, C.R.F. (Newcastle) 35

Thoburn W. (builder; Amble) 13

Thoburn, Jas. (rope makers; S.Blyth) 148

Thompson A. (Sunderland) 86

Thompson, Chris. (Whitby) 104

Thompson, Enoch D. (s.o.; S.Shields) 161

Thompson, Geo. (plumber; Alnwick) 14

Thompson, Geo. (postman; Warkworth) 123

Thompson, Jas. (s.o., draper; Felton) 23, 24

Thompson, Jos.L. (s.o.; S.Shields) 161

Thompson, Matt. (grocer; Warkworth) 30

Thompson, Robt. (Warkworth) 108

Thompson, Wm. (plumber; Blyth) 65

Thompson, Wm. (baker; Monkwearmouth) 84

Thorpe, Wm. (fish merchant, Hartlepool) 115·5.

Tindal, Thos. (pot maker; Seaton Sluice) 134

Tindle, Thos. (m.m.; West Hartlepool) 92

Tomlin, Wm. (Limehouse) 140

Turnbull, John (m.m., s.o.; Amble) 57, 58, 60, 150, 172

Turnbull, Thos. (s.o.; Amble) 57, 58, 60, 137, 150

Turnbull, Wm. (m.t.; Alnwick) 14

Turnbull, Wm. (s.o.; Amble) 150

Turner, John (s.o.; Amble) 74

Turner, John (m.o.; Blyth) 146

Turner, John M.D. (draper; Amble) 67, 85

Tweddle, Margaret (Birmingham) 108

Tyne Iron S.B. Co. (Willington Quay) 129

Tyne Wherry Co. (Newcastle) 129

Tyzack, Samuel (s.o.; Sunderland) 154, 155

United Alkali Co. (Liverpool) 129

Urwin, Robt. (butcher; Newcastle) 37, 120

Vane, Henry (London) 159

Vane, Henry B. (London) 159

Vane, Wm.H. (London) 159

Wake, Benj. (gardener; Morpeth) 152

Wake, Ralph (m.m.; Alnmouth) 135

Walker, Jas. (s.o.; Sunderland) 35

Walker, Jas. (m.m.; Walker) 35

Walker, John (s.b.; Glasgow) 2

Walker, Thos. (Amble) 132

Wallace, Jas. (Blyth) 164

Walton, Geo. (m.m.; Sunderland) 138

Walton, John (painter; Middlesex) 39

Walton, Robt. (m.m.; N.Shields) 39

Ward, Thos. (s.o.; Bridlington) 134

Wardle, Thos. (butcher; Warkworth) 30

Watkins, Hugh (m.m.; Llanarvoy) 10

Watson, John H. (s.o.; Sunderland) 146

Watson, Jos. (m.m.; Sunderland) 47

Watson, Thos.F. (London) 171

Watson, Wm. (s.o.; Seaham Harbour) 92

Watson, Wm. (London) 171

Watson, Wm. H. (s.o.; Sunderland) 146

Watts, Edmund H. (s.br.; Blyth) 137, 172

Weatherill, Wm. (Whitby) 69

Weddell, Robt. (m.t.; Alnwick) 148

Weddon, Thos. (London) 8

Weir, Thos. (block & mast maker; Sunderland) 145

White, Andrew (s.o.; Bishopwearmouth) 84

White, Andrew (Sunderland) 115

White, John (s.o.; Bishopwearmouth) 84

White, Richard (s.o.; Bishopwearmouth) 84

Whiteman, Daniel (m.m.; Alnmouth) 151

Whitfield, Edward (coal fitter, s.o.; Amble) 23, 24, 150

Whitfield, Edward (agent, m.t.; Newcastle) 79, 150

Whitstable Shipping Co. (Whitstable) 74

Wlkie, Jas. (Blyth) 132

Wilkin, Alan (iron monger; Newcastle) 115

Wilkin, Geo. (s.o.; Monkwearmouth) 4

Wilkin, Jas. (iron m.t.; Newcastle) 115

Wilkin, Thos. (flour dealer, m.t.; Newcastle) 37, 120

Wilkinson, Chas.J. (m.t.; London [*died c1843*]) 46

Wilkinson, Edward (Blyth) 164

Wilkinson, Henry (corn m.t.; Alnmouth & High Buston) 105, 148

Wilkinson, John (corn m.t.; High Buston) 77, 105, 148

Willcocks, Chas. (Plymouth) 54

Willis, Thos. H. (miller; Lesbury) 78

Wilson, John (builder; Lesbury) 14

Wilson, Michael (engineer; Amble) 61

Winship, Wm. (Cowpen) 75

Winspeare, John (s.w., Hartlepool) 115·5.

Wood W. (Faversham) 86

Wood, John (colliery owner; Wigham) 14

Wood, Nicholas (farmer, s.o.; Felton) 23, 24

Wood, Wm. (m.m.; Amble & Alnwick) 50, 114

Woodger, John (m.f.; Yarmouth) 146

Wraith, Thos. (agent; Pelaw) 150

Wright, Wm. (m.t.; Sulina) 68

Young, Alex. (Amble) 165

Young, Chas. O. (N. Shields) 5

Young, Jas. (s.o.; S. Shields) 11

Young, John (Alnmouth & Alnwick) 130, 149

Young, Mary (widow; Blyth) 106

Young, Robt. (London) 46

Young, Robt. (wharfinger; Alnmouth [*died c1830*]) 130, 149

Young, Thos. (inn keeper, s.o.; Amble) 78, 146

Young, Thos. (m.m.; Blyth [*died c1840*]) 106

Zacevich, Giuseppe (Lussinpiccolo) 24

Zealand, John (s.o.; Sunderland) 155

Masters

Masters names are followed by the Index Number (as given in the *Fleet List)* of the ship they commanded.

Adler 123
Adler, R. 138
Alder, Robt. 177
Anderson 100
Anderson, John 34
Anderson, Thos. 62
Armstrong, Joseph 11
Asplin, John 16
Atkinson, Thos. 138
Audison, Alex. 59
Bain, Robt. 17, 127
Barrie, Robt. 50
Bell, John 161
Brown, Geo. 59
Brown, John 166
Brown, Thos. 125
Brown, Wm. 162
Buckham, Robt. 166
Burnett, Chas. 139
Calvert Wm. 59
Campbell, James 16
Charlton, Thos. 153
Chesney 21
Chisholm 123
Clark 85
Clarke, Wm. 34
Claxton, John 138, 169
Collard V. 49
Cooper, Wm. 27
Coulson 160, 167
Coulson R. 113
Cowans, Jas. 134
Crossman, Wm. 8
Curry 30
Dagleish, John 107
Darling 121

Darling, John 45
Davidson, Andrew 39
Davidson, Samuel 124
Davis 72
Davison, Ralph 55, 164
Davison, Jos. 130
Dawson, Robt. 171
Dennison, Jos. 69
Dichburn 20
Ditchburn, David 54, 99
Dixon 93
Douglas, Thos. 83
Dowie, Robt. 141
Dunn, Chas. 162
Duthie 67
Emmerson, John 6
Farquhar, Thos. J. 111
Fawcus, Thos. 82
Finney E. 144
Foggin 138
Foster, Jas. 46
Frederick, John 48
Gair, Wm. 143
Galle 14
Galley, John 134
Gibb 146
Gibb, Edward 102
Gibb, Geo. 156
Gibb, Henry 2, 17, 99
Gibb, John H. 61, 76
Gibb, Robt. 130
Gibson, John 126
Glindining, Jas. 34
Gray, Geo. 125
Gray, Henry 125
Greenfield, John 125

Grey, Henry 53
Hardie 3
Harrison, Thos. 134
Hart R. 117
Hay, Jas. 149
Heatley 145
Heatley, Andrew 29, 79
Heatley, Henry 51, 79
Heatley, Jas. 72
Heatly, Henry 91, 156
Hedley 51
Hedley, Henry 105
Hedley, Robt. 142
Henderson, 15, 19
Henderson J. 52
Hogg 65
Hogg, Thos. 107
Holmes, Geo. 47
Hopper, Thos. 139, 140
Howitt, Thos. S. 89
Huntress 148
Jackson 68, 74
James, Benj. 65
Johnson, Geo. 105, 130
Jones E. 10
Kirkwood, Wm. 16
Leighton, Thos. 118
Lewis 109
Lewis, R. 113, 145
Lewis, Robt. 32, 42, 56
Liddle, Geo. 26, 39
Lindsay, John 16, 87, 107
Lodge, J. 90
Lowrey, Robt. 134
Malloch, John 124
Mann 136

Mann, Isaac C. 108
Mann, Robt. 93
Margent, Robt. 130
Marr, Geo. 27
Marshall, Geo. 151
Mather, N. 78
Mather 160
Matthews J. 157
Mattison, John 107, 148
May, John 14
McDonald 108
McIntern, Robt. 17
Meehap 128
Miles 109
Miller, David 34
Milne, Thos. 125
Mitchell, Fred. 153
Moddrel, Jas. 44
Moddril, Jas. 130
Modrel, Jas. 148
Moone, David 59
Moor, Wm. 7
Morn, Jas. 70
Muers, Henry 162
Muers, John 162
Muras, John 92, 107
Murdock, John 140
Newton, Anthony 112
Nicholls H. 52
Parker, Cuthbert 37
Pattison, Ralph 107
Phillips, Jas. 153
Phillips, John 120, 153, 166
Poad, Dennis 34
Poad, Wm. 34

Poole 75
Porritt, Jas. 156
Porter 54
Potter, Geo. 6, 31
Pringle 109
Quack, Wm. 93
Reay, Richard 35
Redpath J. 115·5
Reed, Chas. 167
Rendell, Hugh 134
Richards, Thos. 93
Richardson, Robt. 17, 123, 153
Robertson, Jas.149
Robinson, 3
Robson, Wm. 27
Rochester, Robt. 142
Rochester, Thos. 8
Rowcliff, E. 144
Scott, Wm. 124
Sharp, Lawrence 17
Sheet, Thos. 93
Sheriff, J. 32
Simpson, Matt. 71
Sirvan Geo. 59
Skury, John 118
Smith, Adam 35
Smith, Duncan 19
Smith, Geo. 124
Smith, Jas. 38
Smith, John 100, 101, 126
Stanton, Geo. 130, 153
Stanton, Geo. J. 99
Starling, Wm. 79
Stevens 94

Steward, Thos. 140
Straker, Jas. 26, 153
Straughan, John 82
Surtees, Geo. 38
Swan, Geo. 70, 130
Taylor, Edward 112
Thompson, Jas. 107
Thompson, John 12
Thompson, Thos. 125
Todd E. 1
Trail, John 19
Trail, John P. 14
Tuck, Edward 163
Turnbull 172
Turnbull, John 57
Veitch 86
Wake, Ralph 135
Walker 57
Walker, Richard 59
Walker, Wm. 70
Walton, Robt. 39
Wandless J. 9
Waringer 65
Watson 120
Watson, Jos. 47
Weatherly, Robt. 91
Welch, John 107
Wheatley 93
Whiteman, Daniel 77, 130, 151
Wilkinson, Henry 58
Wilson 9
Wilson, Richard 153
Young, Robt. G. 10
Young, T. 78

Shipbuilders

About 60 of the 172 sailing vessels recorded in the *Fleet List* appear to have been acquired as newly built tonnage for their Aln and Coquet owners. Here is a breakdown of where the new ships came from:

Place of Build	Number	Registered Tons	Average Tonnage
Wear	37	10392	280·86
Amble	8	1479	147·90
Blyth	7	1026	146·57
Tyne	4	572	143·00
Aberdeen	2	162	81·00
Dundee	1	55	55·00
Seaham	1	294	294·00

The large proportion built on the Wear serves as a reminder of that river's tremendous output in the era of the Victorian wooden sailing ship. The Wearside shipbuilder James Gardner was much favoured by the Davison family of Alnwick and Andrew Richardson of Amble. They went to him for their fine, deepwater barques *Aydon Forest, Campsie Glen, Kishon, Maid of Aln* and *Meggie Dixon.*

The second-hand tonnage came from a wide variety of ship building centres both at home and abroad. As with the new ships, the Wear was in the lead. Canada made a significant contribution amounting to twelve ships. Hugh Andrews had five Canadian built sailing ships in his fleet, three of these were born on Prince Edward Island.

Explanation of Shipbuilders List

Each shipbuilding area (or builder, if known) is followed by the Index Number
of individual ships, as given in the *Fleet List*

Canada
Gaspe 132
New Brunswick 1, 157
Nova Scotia 12, 37, 95
Prince Edward Island 36, 42,
55, 68, 133

France.
Boulogne Sur Mer 15
Kerity-Paimpol 116

Ireland
Black Sod, County Mayo 161

Prussia
Barth 90

United Kingdom
Aberdeen 135
   Hall A.& Son 6, 75, 99, 141
Alloa 137
Amble 97
   Bergen J. 93
   Douglas D.A. 154
   Leighton T. 118
   Sanderson 147
   Sanderson J. & Leighton T. 3, 9, 54,
76, 123
   Surtees G. 4, 16, 38, 153
Arbroath 110, 119
Ardrossan
Barr & Shearer 128
Barrowstones 17
Berwick 7
Bideford, Devon 150
Blyth 112, 164
   Bowman G.& Drummond T. 31, 72,
78, 126
   Davison J. 34, 148, 162
   Shepherd W. 8
   Stoveld M. 57
Bridport, Dorset 91, 124
Charlestown, Fife 107
Dundee 2, 59, 70, 105

Elie, Fife 77, 79
Fraserburgh 52
Garmouth 62
Glasgow 32
Glasson 92
Grangemouth 13, 151
Howden Dike, Yorkshire 104
Leith 53
Limekilns, Fife 132
Port Downie, Sterling 66
Ramsgate 120
Seaham
   Potts 64
   Culcoates 69
Southampton 142
Southwold, 160.
Stockton, 127, 155.
Tyne 11, 48, 82, 125, 130, 152
   Boutland W. 166
   Brown J. 102
   Gaddy & Lamb 33
   Trotter & Young 39
   Hutchinson 61
   Smith T. & W. 87
   Young T. & Co. 5
Wear 18, 73
   Austin S.P. 129
   Bailey E. 30
   Barkes J. 145, 146
   Briggs J. 131
   Brown E. 140
   Brown J.J. 25
   Brunton J. 84
   Bulmer J. 143
   Burn T. 134
   Candlish R. 170
   Carr H. 117
   Crown J. 44
   Crown W. 60
   Dobinson H. 121
   Douglas D.A. 43, 58
   Doxford & Crown 83
   Forrest P. 63

Appendix I

Arrivals & Departures of Local Ships from Amble

May 1870 to April 1871

Name	Master	Arrived From	Sailed To
May 1870			
Lady Matheson	Lodge	Boulogne	Boulogne
Isabellas	Young	Boulogne	Boulogne
Sun	Lewis	Boulogne	Boulogne
Landscape	Wheatley	Boulogne	Copenhagen
Amble	Wandless	Boulogne	Boulogne
Garibaldi	Nicholls	Sunderland	Dingwall
Percy	Hart	Boulogne	Boulogne
June 1870			
Seaflower	Adler	Boulogne	Boulogne
Isabellas	Young	Boulogne	Boulogne
Percy	Hart	Boulogne	Boulogne
Amble	Wandless	Boulogne	Boulogne
July 1870			
Seaflower	Adler	Boulogne	Boulogne
Isabellas	Young	Boulogne	Boulogne
Sun	Lewis	Boulogne	Boulogne
Amble	Wandless	Boulogne	Boulogne
Percy	Hart	Boulogne	Boulogne
Isabellas	Young	Boulogne	Boulogne
August 1870			
Sun	Lewis	Boulogne	Boulogne
Seaflower	Adler	Boulogne	Schiedam
September 1870			
Amble	Wandless	Boulogne	Calais
Percy	Hart	Boulogne	Boulogne
Sun	Lewis	Boulogne	Boulogne
Seaflower	Adler	Schiedam	Schiedam
Garibaldi	Nicholls	Paisley	N. Sunderland
Isabellas	Young	Boulogne	Boulogne
Percy	Hart	Boulogne	Boulogne
Garibaldi	Nicholls	N. Sunderland	?
Amble	Wandless	Calais	?

October 1870

Garibaldi	Nicholls	N. Sunderland	?
Sun	Lewis	Boulogne	Boulogne
Isabellas	Young	Boulogne	Boulogne
Bonne Mere	Henderson	?	Alnmouth

November 1870

Bonne Mere	Henderson	Alnmouth	?
Seaflower	Adler	Schiedam	Boulogne
Agenoria	Robinson	London	Lisbon
Amble	Wandless	Boulogne	Boulogne
Sun	Lewis	Boulogne	Boulogne
Lady Matherson	Lodge	Lowestoft	Boulogne
Gloriana	Ditchburn	London	Boulogne
Isabellas	Mather	Boulogne	Boulogne
Percy	Hart	Boulogne	Blyth

December 1870

Amble	Wandless	Boulogne	Boulogne
Sun	Wandless	Boulogne	Boulogne
Percy	Hart	Boulogne	Boulogne
Lady Matheson	Lodge	Boulogne	Boulogne

January 1871

Seaflower	Adler	Boulogne	Boulogne
Isabellas	Mather	Boulogne	Boulogne
Landscape	Wheatley	Boulogne	Boulogne
Gloriana	Ditchburn	Boulogne	Boulogne
Sun	Lewis	Boulogne	Boulogne
Amble	Wandless	Boulogne	Boulogne
Lady Matheson	Lodge	Boulogne	Boulogne

February 1871

Percy	Hart	Boulogne	Boulogne
Seaflower	Adler	Boulogne	Boulogne
Percy	Hart	Boulogne	Boulogne

March 1871

Isabellas	Mather	Boulogne	Boulogne
Gloriana	Ditchburn	Boulogne	Boulogne
Sun	Lewis	Boulogne	Boulogne
Amble	Wandless	Boulogne	Boulogne
Lady Matheson	Lodge	Boulogne	Boulogne
Percy	Hart	Boulogne	Boulogne
Seaflower	Adler	Boulogne	Boulogne

April 1871

Isabellas	Mather	Boulogne	Boulogne
Gloriana	Ditchburn	Boulogne	Lubeck
Sun	Lewis	Boulogne	Lubeck
Amble	Wandless	Boulogne	Lubeck
Lady Matheson	Lodge	Boulogne	Norrkoping
Percy	Hart	Boulogne	Boulogne
Garibaldi	Nicholls	London	N. Sunderland
Seaflower	Adler	Boulogne	Boulogne
Isabellas	Young	Boulogne	Boulogne

The port of Boulogne at the turn of the century; a place much visited by the Coquet sailing ships. The vessel in the foreground is the 282 ton Norwegian brig *Andover*. Built at St John, New Brunswick, in the early 1840's, she was rigged down to a hulk in 1906. Eleven of these Canadian built sailing vessels were owned locally. Ahead of the *Andover* lies a square-sterned barque. These pair are typical of the myriads of small, wooden, square-rigged sailing ships which carried so much of the world's trade throughout the Nineteenth Century.
(From an old postcard)

Steamers belonging to Hugh Andrews (Amble's most prominent ship-owner), North-East companies with which he was associated and their successors.

Registered as belonging to Hugh Andrews:

WARKWORTH (1871-1875)

218 gross 149 net tons   136 x 20·2 x 9·5 feet

Engine: ?, 2-cylinder, 40 h.p., by Clark Watson Eng.

17.7.1871: Launched by Wigham Richardson, Wallsend, for Hugh Andrews. *1875:* A. de Ysasi, Bilboa; re-named *Maria. 1885:* re-named *Palmira. 1886:* No longer listed in *Lloyd's Register.*

The *Warkworth* of 1874.

WARKWORTH (1874-1880)   O/N 70228

426 gross 334 net tons   160·8 x 27·1 x 12·9 feet

Engine: Compound, 2-cylinder, by Christie, Gutch & Co., North Shields.

1874: Completed by C.S. Swan, Wallsend, for Hugh Andrews. *1880:* Les Fils de T. Conseil, Bordeaux; re-named *Theodore Conseil. 1899:* Shipping Investments Ltd. (C.H. Pile, mgr), London; re-named *Warkworth. 1901:* A.W. Proctor & Co., London. *1902:* Bouchard & Bros., Quebec; re-named *Gaspesien. 1910:* Gaspe Bay Chaleur S.S. Line (Phidelem Blouin), Quebec. *1917:* Canadian Maritime Co. Ltd., Canada. *1919:* A.A. Capparis, Greece; re-named *Olympos. 1922:* G. Gromann, Piraeus. *1924:* Mrs A. Tagaris (T. Tagaris, mgr.), Piraeus; re-named *Panayotis. 1925:* Omer Luftiy Bey, Izmir; re-named *Luftiye. 1931:* Mahmut Luftiy, Izmir. *5.2.1932:* Wrecked near Bender Eregil (Black Sea) while on ballast passage from Eregil to Istanbul.

BROOMHILL (1878-1908)   O/N 78687
638 gross 398 net tons   174·7 x 29·0 x 12·8 feet
Engine: Compound Inverted, 2-cylinder, 95 h.p., by builders.
1878: Built by T. Wingate & Co., Glasgow. *1878*: H. Andrews (34/64),
Felton, & R. Taylor (30/64), Dundee. *21.3.1888*: John Park, Amble, appointed managing
owner.*21.2.1890*: Hugh Andrews became sole owner. *24.12.1897*: Broomhill Shipping Co.,
Newcastle. *31.12.1897*: Richard Jack, Newcastle, appointed manager. *31.12.1900*: Broomhill
Collieries Ltd., Newcastle. *21.1.1901*: Montague Frances Maclean, Newcastle, appointed
ships husband. *26.9.1908:* Furness Whithy & Co., Hartlepool, and in same year to the Lon-
don Welsh Steamship Co. Ltd. (Robert T. Thompson & Percy I. Clark), London; re-named
Cardiff Trader. *1914:* Steam Traders Ltd., London; re-named *Luffmore*. *1916:* S. Greaves,
Goole. *1923:* Broken up in Germany.

WARKWORTH HARBOUR (1880-1882)   O/N 79238
439 net 694 gross tons   180·4 x 30 x 13 feet
Engine: Compound, 2-cylinder, 85 h.p., by Dunsmuir & Jackson, Glasgow.
1880: Built Paisley by H. M'Intyre., for Hugh Andrews. *12.9.1881:* John Park, Warkworth
Harbour, appointed manager. *10.4.1882:* Tyne Steam Shipping Co., Newcastle; re-named
Warkworth. *1903:* Tyne Tees Steam Shipping Company. *1913:* G. Germano, Italy, re-named
Mariannina. *1919:* M. Cormio, Italy. *1923:* No longer listed in *Lloyd's Register*.

Warkworth Shipping Co. Ltd. (H. Andrews), Newcastle:

CORNHILL (1891-1898)   O/N 97958
922 gross 534 net tons   193·7 x 31·5 x 15·1 feet
Engines: Triple expansion, 3-cylinder, 99 h.p., by builders.
1891: Completed by R. Stephenson & Co. Ltd., Hebburn, for Warkworth Shipping Co.
1898: G.regory B. Wadsworth, Goole. *1919:* Llewellyn Shipping Co. Ltd. (W.B. Thomas &
Co. Ltd.), Goole. *1923:* F. L. Nimtz, Stettin, re-named *Marianne*. *1930:* F. Pekerns & Co.,
Ventspils, re-named *Aina*. *1932*: Dismantled.

Danehill Steam Ship Co. (H. Andrews), Newcastle:

DANEHILL (1884-1898)   O/N 91152
1124 gross 721 net tons   220·5 x 35·1 x 13·7 feet
Engines: Compound, 2-cylinder, 125 h.p. by Wallsend Slipway Co., Ltd., Newcastle.
1884: Built by Campbell, Mackintosh & Boustead, Elswick, Newcastle., for Danehill Steam
Ship Co. *1898:* Ostlandske Lloyd (Rolf Andvard), Christiania, Norway; re-named *Memento*.
1906: A/S Ganger Rolf (Fred Olsen), Norway. *31 March 1916:* Struck mine and sunk near
Pakefield Gat Bouy when bound from London towards Porsgrund with coke.

Broomhill Coal Co., Broomhill Collieries Ltd., & Broomhill Steamships Ltd:

> In November 1900, Hugh Andrews mining and shipping concerns (including the
> control of Amble Harbour) became part of the mushrooming shipping, shipbuild-
> ing and industrial empire spearheaded by the Hartlepool entrepreneur Sir Chris-
> topher Furness. Thereafter the ships were owned by Broomhill Collieries Ltd.,
> and later, Broomhill Steamships Ltd., who had offices in Newcastle.

The *Turrethill* lying alongside at Amble.
(Courtesy: Ron French)

TURRETHILL (1895-1913)   O/N 104281
690 gross   419 net tons   195 x 31 x 12·5 feet
Engine: Compound, 2-cylinder, 95 h.p., by builders.
Capacity: 1070 tons.
1895: Built at Sunderland by William Doxford & Sons for Broomhill Coal Co. *12.6.1895:*
Trials. As soon as these were completed she   proceeded to Amble to load. *1913:* Sold to
Foster Bros., Newcastle. *13.5.1914:* Capsized and sunk off Southwold, while on passage
from Goole towards Poole with coal, with the loss of several of her crew and the master's
son.

> The *Turrethill* was the smallest, by a considerable margin, of some 176 "turret"
> steamers built by Doxford's between the years 1892 and 1911. According to the
> *Marine Engineer* of 1895, she was the first vessel of this type to be: "built for the
> coal coasting trade, and, should the venture be a success, its promoters intend to
> adapt that class of vessel in their transport of coal from Amble to the southern
> ports." The experiment must not have turned out as well as expected. No more
> "turret" ships were acquired by the company.
>   "Turret" ships, although of peculiar appearance, offered certain advantages in
> design and operational economies which were attractive to shipowners. The last of
> them was the Spanish owned *Nuestra Senora del Carmen* which was wrecked in
> 1963. She was then sixty-eight years old. A few years before the author had seen
> her lying off Vittoria , Brazil, waiting to load iron-ore.

BROOMHILL (1909-1917)   O/N 125460
1392 gross 843 net tons   243·2 x 36 x 14·6 feet
Engine: Triple expansion, 3-cylinder, 170 h.p., by Richardson, Westgarth & Co., West Hartlepool.
1909: Built West Hartlepool by Irvines Shipbuilding & Dry Docks Co., for Broomhill Coal Co. *10.5.1917:* Captured and sunk by explosive charges set by *UC61* in 50°25' N., 2°32' W., when on passage from Penarth to Sheerness with coal.

BONDICAR (1910-1947)   O/N 129741
1441 gross 804 net tons   240·3 x 36·5 x 14·4 feet
Engine: Triple expansion, 3-cylinder, 182 h.p., by Richardson Westgarth & Co., Sunderland.
23.12.1909: Launched at Sunderland by J. Crown & Sons Ltd., for Broomhill Coal Co. *15.9.1918:* Attacked by submarine in Bristol Channel. Torpedo missed. *1930:* Heavy weather crossing from Hamburg to Tyne. Took six days instead of usual 42 hours. *1934:* Stranded on Danish Coast in bad position. Subsequently re-floated. *1947:* Cia. Atala de Nav. General, Ltda., Panama. re-named *Chryssoula*. Later *Hellenic Chryssoula*. *Autum 1952*: Laid up at Cardiff. *4.6.1954*: Arrived Newport, Mon., for breaking up following sale to John Cashmore.

AXWELL (1912-1917)   O/N 127448
1442 gross 784 net tons   240·2 x 36·4 x 14·3 feet
Engine: Triple expansion, 3-cylinder, 182 h.p. by Richardson, Westgarth & Co., Sunderland.
19.8.1909: Launched at Sunderland by J. Crown & Son for Furness Withy & Company (Stephen W. Furness), West Hartlepool. *1912:* Transferred to Broomhill Collieries Ltd. *13.11.1917:* Torpedoed and sunk three miles W.S.W. from the Owers Light Vessel by *UB56* while on passage from Amble to Rouen with coal. Two lives were lost.

TOGSTON (1909-1913)   O/N 129737
1057 gross 633 net 1550 d.w tons.   210·4 x 33·1 x 13·5 feet
Engine: Triple expansion, 3-cylinder, 105 h.p. by Richardson, Westgarth & Co., Sunderland.
28.9.1909: Launched at Sunderland by Osbourne, Graham & Co., to order of Furness, Withy & Company, West Hartlepool, for Broomhill Collieries. *21.10.1909*: Trials. *1913*: Transferred to G.V. Turnbull & Company, Leith, and later in same year to Furness Whithy & Company, West Hartlepool. *1.6.1915:* Acquired by South Metropolitan Gas Company, London. *21.10.1915:* Arrived Tyne for repairs at Cleland's Graving Dock following a collision in the Thames estuary with the steamer *Amsteldam* which also belonged to the South Metropolitan Gas Company. This vessel arrived in the Tyne on the same day as the *Togston* for repairs at Smith's Pontoon Dock. *18.10.1917:* Torpedoed and sunk in North Sea in 53°40' N., 00°12' E by *UC47* when on passage from Tyne to London with coal.

BROOMHILL (1921-1927)   O/N 145281
1247 gross 684 net tons.   234 x 34·7 x 14·9 feet
Engine: Twin screw, Triple expansion, 6-cylinder, 84 h.p., by builders.
1914: Built at Kiel by Howaldtswerke as *Alsen*.
The early career of this vessel is unclear although suggestions have been made that she was employed as a collier by the German Navy during World War I. Ceded to Britain as a reparation and acquired in 1921 by Broomhill Collieries. *1922/23 Lloyd's Register*: Describes her as ex-*Alsen, Fehmarn* and notes that: "this vessel, which was not classed in another register, has now been surveyed by the Surveyors of *Lloyd's Register* and a certificate for six months issued." *1927*: E. Halm & Company, Germany, re-named *Lotte Halm*. *14.8.1941:* Bombed and sunk off Nordeney.

AMBLE (1921-1939)   O/N 69560
1162 gross 681 net   230·7 x 34·3 x 13·2 feet
Engine: Triple expansion, 3-cylinder, 120 h.p., by builders.
11.2.1920: Launched at Amsterdam by Verschure & Co., as *Laura* for the Holland Gulf
Steam Navigation Co., Rotterdam. *1921:* Acquired by Broomhill Colleries for about
£17,250; re-named *Amble. 23.10.1922:* Badly damaged following a collision in the Kaiser
Wilhelm Canal with the Danish steamer *Danefelt. 20.12.1925:* Grounded near Alnmouth during a gale. *30.12.1925:* Re-floated. Leaking badly, had to be put ashore at Amble for temporary repairs. *3.1.1926:* Taken to Tyne for repairs by Smith's Dock Co., North Shields.
16.12.1939: Struck mine in 54°55' N., 1°30' W when on passage from London towards
Amble. *Lloyd's War Losses* gives positions) of loss as 54° 52' N., 0 °48' W., or 54° 52' N.,
51° 30' W., and notes: "Drifted ashore; Re-floated & towed to Sunderland Dec 25. Broken
up."

CHEVINGTON (1923-1941)   O/N 145524
1537 gross 920 net   244·8 x 38 x 17·5 feet
Engine: Triple expansion, 3-cylinder, 150 h.p., by Earle's Co., Ltd., Hull
1923: Built at Haverton Hill-on-Tees by the Furness Shipbuilding Co., for Broomhill Colleries. *15.5.1925:* Collided with collier *Corcrest* in the Long Reach, River Thames. Both
damaged. *12.10.1941:* Torpedoed and sunk by an E-boat in 59°59' N., 1°52' E., when bound
from London towards Grangemouth with 2,350 tons of cement. Seven of her crew and two
gunners were lost. *Lloyd's War Losses* notes: "Wreck lies in 53 18 N., 1 50 24 E."

TOGSTON (1924-1941)   O/N 148071
1547 gross 898 net tons   245·4 x 38·6 x 15·5 feet
Engine: Triple expansion, 3-cylinder, 166 h.p., by North East Marine Engineering Co.
17.4.1924: Launched at Haverton Hill-on-Tees by Furness Shipbuilding Co., for Broomhill
Colleries. *8.3.1941:* Torpedoed and sunk by an E-boat two miles from Smith's Knoll when
bound from Blyth towards London with 2,200 tons coal. Eight of her 19 man crew were lost.

HAUXLEY (1925-1941)   O/N 149404
1595 gross 937 net tons   245·6 x 39·4 x 19·1 feet
Engine: Triple expansion, 3-cylinder, 163 h.p., by G. Clark, Ltd., Sunderland.
30.11.1925: Launched at Haverton Hill-on-Tees by Furness Shipbuilding Co., for Broomhill
Collieries. *17.10.1941:* Torpedoed by E-Boat six miles N.N.W., of Smith's Knoll with loss of
one life when on passage from London towards Amble. Taken in tow, she sank the following
day in 50°3' 30" N., 1°35' 30" E.

Tugs owned by Hugh Andrews, companies with which he was associated and their successors:

PACTOLUS (1876-1885)   O/N 60561
Wood paddle tug.
93 gross 17 net tons   7·2 x 17·9 x 9·6 feet
Engine: Side lever, 1-cylinder, 38 h.p., by J. R. Scott, North Shields..
1870: Built by Charles W. Dogin, North Shields, for Thompson Johnson Newton & Co.,
North Shields. *5.2.1874:* John F.F. Common & Co., North Shields. *3.8.1875:* John Sowers,
Dublin. *1876:* Hugh Andrews. *1885:* Irving Steam Tug Co., Sunderland.

114

PORTHILL (1886-1909)   O/N 84675
Iron paddle tug.
83 gross 26 net tons   7·7 x 17·2 x 8·7 feet
Engine: 60 h.p., 10 knots.
1882: Built South Shields by J.T. Eltringham.
1882: Robert Lee, Cardiff. *1886:* Hugh Andrews. *7.9.1909:* Sold to Greek owners for £520.
No further trace.

COQUET (c1892-1899)   O/N 101802
Iron paddle tug.
119 gross 12 net tons   90·3 x 19·2 x 9·4 feet
Engines: Lever, 2-cylinder, 45 h.p., by builders.
1892: Built South Shields by J.P. Rennoldson.
1896: H. Andrews. 1899: T. Gray & Co., Hull; re-named *Frenchman.* 1906: Re-built and
lengthened.. 1921: United Towing Co., Hull. 1928: Withdrawn from service. 1929: Engine
re-moved; reduced to barge. 1968: Broken up.

STANLEY (1911-1913)   O/N 109371
Steel paddle tug.
164 gross 34 net tons   108·3 x 18·8 x 10 feet
Engine: 60 h.p. by Hepple & Co., South Shields.
1900: Built South Shields by J.T. Eltringham for John Dent, Newcastle. *1911:* Broomhill
Collieries (Manager: James Earnshaw, Warkworth Harbour Office, Amble). *20.11.1913:*
Crown Agents for West Africa (Government of Nigeria). *After 1918/1919*: No longer listed
in *Lloyd's Register.*

PALMERSTON (c1923-1927)   O/N 44923
Iron paddle tug.
121 gross 28 net tons   96·5 x 18·5 x 9·4 feet
Engine: Lever, 2-cylinder, 60 h.p., by builders.
1864: Built Cubitt Town, London, by Simpson & Co., for Dover Harbour Board. *1883:*
Great Western Railway Co., Paddington, London, employed at Fishguard. *c1923:* Broomhill
Colleries. *3.3.1927:* Sold to ship-breakers

AYR (c1926-1947)   O/N 104796
Iron paddle tug
124 gross 14 net tons   90 x 19·1 x 9·2 feet
Engines: Lever. 2-cylinder, 50 h.p., by builders.
1897: Built South Shields by J.P. Rennoldson & Sons for Ayr Harbour Trustees, Ayr. *c1926:*
Broomhill Coal Co. *1947:* National Coal Board. *20.10.1949:* J.J. King, Gateshead, for breaking up.

Following the breaking up of the *Ayr,* a standard World War II built screw tug,
the *TID 66,* was transferred from the Coal Board to the Warkworth Harbour
Board. Early in 1963 she left the Coquet for to be re-fitted on the Clyde, for service at Benghazi, but never made it. After two break downs, in the North Sea, she
put into Leith and was subsequently broken up.

Steam Yachts owned by Hugh Andrews and listed with the Royal Yacht Squadron:

Hugh Andrews was elected a member of the Royal Yacht Squadron in 1893 and remained so until his death in 1926. At least four of his yachts were named *Taurus*.

TAURUS (1898-1899)   O/N 93468
ex *Theodora.*
477·57 gross 267·7 net 546 tons Thames measurement.   165 x 27·3 x 14 feet
Engine: Triple expansion, 3-cylinder, 90 h.p., by builders.
Designer: J.H. Ritchie.
1887: Built at Dundee by Gourlay Bros. & Co.

TAURUS (1901-1906)   O/N 112789
ex *Eros.*
564·71 gross 289·61 net 770 tons Thames measurement.   228·3 x 26·8 x 15·4 feet
Engine: Compound inverted, 2-cylinder, 230 h.p. by Day & Summers, Southampton.
Designer: A.H. Brown.
1885: Built at Erith by Shuttleworth & Chapman.

TAURUS (1909-1913)   O/N 81644
ex *Aline.*
229·29 gross 155·92 net 373 tons Thames measurement.   165·7 x 22·1 x 11·5 feet
Engine: Compound Inverted, 2-cylinder, 61 h.p., by Walker Henderson & Co., Glasgow.
Designer: W. Connel.
1880: Built at Leith by Ramage & Ferguson.

VERONA (1914-1916)   O/N 98849
ex *Tighnamara*
330·62 gross 156·43 net 437 tons Thames measurement.   165·5 x 24·1 x 14·1 feet
Engine: Inverted, 4-cylinder, 133 h.p., by builders.
Designed by builders.
1890: Built Paisley by Fleming & Ferguson.
7.11.1914: Hired as auxiliary patrol yacht by Royal Navy. Served in Peterhead and Cromarty areas. *24.2.1917:* Struck mine and sunk off Portmahomack.

CALA MARA (1922)   O/N 99942
ex *Seanymph* ex *Jeanette*
216·82 gross 81·97 net 313 tons Thames measurement.   152·5 x 21·15 x 11·1 feet
Engine: Triple expansion, 3-cylinder, 64 h.p., by builders.
Designer: St. C.J. Byrne.
1898: Built Barrow by Vickers, Sons & Maxim Ltd.

Prior to becoming a member of the Royal Yacht Squadron, Hugh Andrews owned the following iron built steam yacht:

TAURUS   O/N 76877

200·76 gross 136·52 net 317 tons yacht measurement   143 x 22 x 10·3 feet.
Engine: Compound Surface Condensing, 60 h.p., 10·5 knots
1876: Built Barrow.

An inventory of this vessel notes that she had: "...a roomy deck-house upholstered in cretonne, with velvet curtains, and below has a large saloon fitted in mahogany and maple. Painted and decorated in gold and other rich colours in oil, handsomely upholstered, and many conveniently arranged and well-fitted cabins; owner's cabin, containing two beds, is by special arrangement of copper coil with adjustable valve heated by steam, the usual store rooms, offices, baths, w.c.'s, &c., and accommodation for crew abaft the engines."

The *Taurus* had a dynamo manufactured by Holmes & Son, of Newcastle, which produced electricity sufficient to light the saloons and cabins at all times. She was still afloat, just before World War I, under the name *The Lady of Clennel,* belonging to Anthony Wilkinson of London.

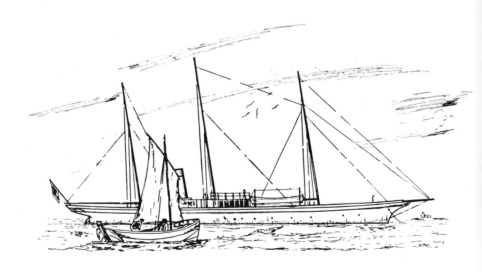

The elegant *Taurus,* built in 1876

Appendix III

Sailing Ship Rigs

The classification of sailing ships rigs and rigging is a contentious one which has exercised a lot of minds in recent years. There were many variations to a theme, particularly in respect of the smaller vessels which were often rigged as their owners, or masters, wanted them - what was one man's sloop was another man's smack or cutter. Our maritime forebears did not seem unduly concerned about the minutiae of rig classification. In the course of a long career a ship could carry two or three different rigs. This may have been brought about after a dismasting or for economic reasons. The masts, spars and sails of a wrecked, laid up, or discarded ship were often used in the refit of active vessels.

As a general rule, from about the second quarter of the Nineteenth Century, British registered merchant sailing ships were classified according to rig. This was entered on their Custom House Registers, in the listings of *Lloyd's Register of Shipping* and other directories of that genre. Ten different types of rig were represented amongst the Aln and Coquet vessels. There were something like 43 brigs; 38 snows; 30 barques; 27 schooners; 15 sloops; 10 brigantines; 2 smacks and full-rigged ships; 1 schooner-brig, 1 fore-and-aft schooner and one 3-masted topsail schooner.

Following, is an explanation of these various rigs as understood by the author. They may vary in some minor details from the definitions used in "tall ship" and yachting circles of the present day.

Ship or full-rigged ship: Three or more masts. Square-rigged on all masts. The Aln & Coquet full-rigged-ships were three masted.

Barque: Three or more masts. Square-rigged on all masts except the aftermost which was fore-and-aft rigged. All of the Aln/Coquet barques were three masted.

Brig: Two masts. Square-rigged on each mast.

Snow: Two masts. Identical to brig except that a try-sail mast was fitted abaft the main-mast from which the spanker was set. To the seafaring communities of the Nineteenth Century the types appear to have been lumped together and described as brigs.

Brigantine: Two masts. Square-rigged on fore-mast; fore-and-aft on main.

Schooner-brig: Two masts. Probably similar to brigantine, perhaps with a spencer sail set abaft the fore-mast.

Schooner: Two masts. Both fore-and-aft rigged with square top-sails on the fore-mast.

Fore-and-aft schooner: Two masts. Both fore-and-aft rigged.

3-mast top-sail schooner: Fore-and-aft rigged on all three masts with square sail, or sails, on fore-top-mast.

Sloop and Sloop with Running Bowsprit: One mast. Fore-and-aft rigged. Some would have almost certainly carried a square top-sail.

Smack: A general classification applied to many small trading and fishing vessels rather than a particular rig. Many would have been rigged as sloops.

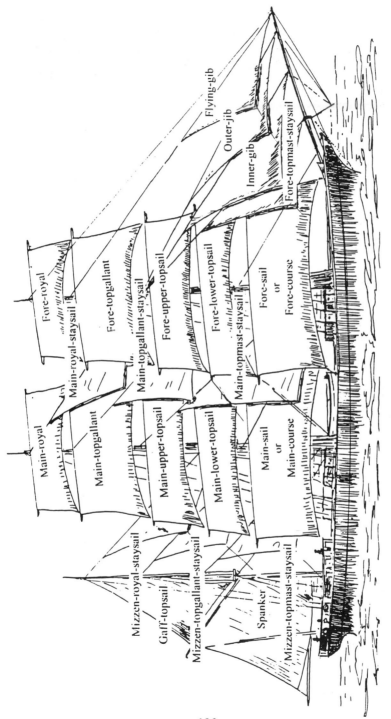

Flying-jib

Outer-jib

Inner-jib

Fore-topmast-staysail

Fore-royal

Main-royal-staysail

Fore-topgallant

Main-topgallant-staysail

Fore-upper-topsail

Fore-lower-topsail

Main-topmast-staysail

Fore-sail
or
Fore-course

Main-royal

Main-topgallant

Main-upper-topsail

Main-lower-topsail

Main-sail
or
Main-course

Mizzen-royal-staysail

Gaff-topsail

Mizzen-topgallant-staysail

Spanker

Mizzen-topmast-staysail

The Sails of a North Country Barque of the 1870's.
(Drawing by R.E. Keys)

Glossary

Armstrong's Patent: Does not allude to any registered patent or to the distinguished Newcastle entrepreneur of "Armstrong's factory" fame. It was a term used to describe any apparatus (the anchor windlass in particular) in use aboard a sailing ship which required hard manual labour - "a strong arm" - to operate.

Ballast: In the case of the Aln and Coquet sailing vessels, it was some heavy material, such as stone, carried in the bottom of the hold to give stability when sailing without cargo. Nowadays water ballast is carried in "deep" or "double bottom" tanks.

Collier: Name given to a vessel, sail or powered, regularly employed in the carriage of coal.

Cutwater: A piece of timber bolted to the foreside of the stem which "cut the water."

Dog watch: Two half watches, of two hours each, into which the period from 4 p.m., to 8 p.m., is divided.

Donkey's breakfast: A merchant seaman's mattress which was usually filled with straw.

Fathom: A unit of measurement (6 feet or 1·829 meters) used for measuring lengths of cordage and depth of water.

Fo'c'sle or forecastle: A raised structure, above the upper deck, leading aft from the stem. It is also the generic term used to indicate the living space of the crew which, in sailing ships, was usually in the fore part of the vessel.

Mulie-rigged barge: Rigged like a ketch but with the type of spritsail commonly seen on Thames barges set from the main mast.

Prize: An enemy vessel captured at sea, or seized in port, after the outbreak of war.

Shipbroker: An agent who acts for a shipowner to secure cargoes, negotiate the sale and purchase of ships, and any other business connected with the shipping industry.

Shipwright: A skilled artisan who performs the practical work of putting together the fastenings and various parts of a ship. In the days of the small wooden merchantman he was commonly the ship builder.

Spencer: A fore-and-aft sail, similar to the spanker, set from any mast of a square-rigged vessel except the aftermost. Not all square-rigged ships carried this sail.

Studding sail or stunsail: A sail set outside a square sail which serves to extend its width and the total sail area. Used only in fine weather. See painting of *Sarah*.

Tramp: A cargo-carrying merchant vessel which is not employed on a regular route. It may pick up or deliver cargo anywhere in the world.

Bibliography

Books

Admiralty, Hydrographic Department, *North Sea Pilot,* Parts II, III & IV (London, 1948-50)

Bateson, E., *A History of Northumberland,* Vol 2 (Newcastle, 1895)

Capricorn Press Pty Ltd., ed., *Antarctica* (Sydney, 1985)

Colledge, J.J., *Ships of the Royal Navy* (Newton Abbot, 1969)

Conrad, J., *The Mirror of the Sea* (London, 1927)

Hope, R., *A New History of British Shipping* (London, 1990)

Hughes, E., and Eames, A., *Porthmadog Ships* (Caernarfon, 1975)

MacGregor, D.R., *Fast Sailing Ships 1775-1875* (Lymington, 1973)

McAndrews, T.L., *Amble and District* (Amble, c. 1910)

McInnes, R.G., *History of Amble* (Amble, 1880)

Maury, M.F., *The Physical Geography of the Sea* (Washington, 1856)

Moffat, H.Y., *From Ship's-Boy to Skipper* (Paisley, 1910)

Morrison, P.G., and Rylance, T., *Amble, the Friendliest Port* (Amble, 1988)

Patrick D., and Geddie W., *Chamber's Concise Gazettere of the World* (London, 1914)

Raper, *Practice of Navigation and Nautical Astronomy* (c. 1875)

Roberts Brian, *Chronological List of Antarctic Expeditions*, reprint from 'Polar Record', Vol 9 (Cambridge, 1958)

Runciman, W., *Collier Brigs and their Sailors* (London, 1926)

Runciman, W., *Sunbeam II in 1930* (Newcastle upon Tyne, 1930).

Shipping Editor at Lloyd's, ed., *Lloyd's Maritime Atlas* (London, 1969)

Simper, R., *North East Sail* (Newton Abbot, 1975)

Talbot-Booth, E.C., ed., *His Majesty's Merchant Navy* (London, 1945)

Tennent, A.J., *British Merchant Ships Sunk by U-Boats in the 1914-1918 War* (Newport, Gwent, 1990)

Wilkinson, D., and Morrison, P.G., *A Story of Amble* (Amble, 1985)

Periodicals

Sea Breezes (Liverpool, since 1919)

Shipbuilding and Shipping Record (London, 1913-30)

Newspapers

Newcastle Journal

Newcastle Daily Journal

Newcastle Courant

Newcastle Chronicle

Index

Index of Vessels

A.B. Gowan (ferry) 28
Aaron Eton 30
Adventure 30, 91
Agenoria 27, 33, 34, 108
Agnes & Louisa (steamer) 57
Aid 24, 27, 34
Ailsa Craig 34
Aina (steamer) 111
Aline (yacht) 116
Alma 40
Alnwick Castle 5, 34
Alnwick Packet 35
Alsen (steamer) 113
Alycon 70, 72
Amazone 41
Amble 27, 35, 107, 108, 109
Amble (steamer) 114
Amity 35
Amphitrite 36
Amsteldam (steamer) 113
Anglo-Mex101 (tug) 28
Ardincaple (steamer) 29
Arethusa 14, 15
Ariel 90
Ashby 36
Auld Reckie 36
Australia (tug) 61
Axwell (steamer) 113
Aydon Forest 14, 36, 37, 104
Ayr (tug) 115
Bondicar (steamer) 113
Bonne Mere 37, 38, 107, 108
Breeze 27, 38
Britannia 38
Broomhill (steamer) 111, 113

Brothers No 2, 51
Calypso, H.M.S. 6
Cala Mara (yacht) 116
Cambria 30
Camperdown 2, 15, 38, 39
Campsie Glen 4, 30, 39, 104
Cardiff Trader (steamer) 111
Caspian 40
Catherine Maria 13
Catherine Tucker 73
Cedar 40
Ceres 40
Ceylon 40, 41
Chaluranga 41
Charles Molloy 41
Chevington Oak 26
Chevington (steamer) 114
Chivington Oak 26
Christina Murray 41
Chryssoula (steamer) 113
Cleveland 41
Collingwood (tug) 4
Comet 54
Coquet (tug) 115
Coral Isle 41, 42
Coral Queen 42
Corcrest (steamer) 114
Cornhill (steamer) 111
Cretebow (tug) 28
Cretestem (tug) 28
Croft 20, 21, 42
Cuba 42
Danefelt (steamer) 114
Danehill (steamer) 111
Derwentwater 24, 42, 43
Diamond 43
Diligence 24

Dorothy 44
Douse 44
Dove 44
Dreadnaught (tug) 89
Duchess of Northumberland 27, 44
E.L.Walton 86
Earl of Newburgh 5, 13, 44, 45
Eastern Province 45
Elbe 45
Electra 45
Eliza Laing 45, 46
Elizabeth 46
Elizabeth Henderson 46
Ellen Browne 74, 94
Ernestine (steamer) 40
Eros (yacht) 116
Esperance 41
Express 5, 6, 20, 46
Express (tug) 62
Fehmarn (steamer) 113
Felix Brandt 45
Felix Ladbroke 46
Ferret (pilot cutter) 89
Ferryhill (motor ship) 25
Fifeshire 62
Frances Western 48
Frenchman (tug) 115
Friends Goodwill 5
Frienship 48
G.L.Wilcox 60
Galilee 48
Gambier 48
Garibaldi 48, 49, 107, 108, 109
Gaspesien (steamer) 110

123

Talisman 82
Taurus (yacht) 93, 116
Telemanchus 13, 82
The Lady of Clennel (yacht) 117
Theodora (yacht) 116
Theodore Conseill (steamer) 116
Thistle 83
Thomas & Isabella 81
Thomas Rusbridger 83
TID 66 (tug) 115
Tighnamara (yacht) 116
Togston (steamer) 113, 114
Tourist (steamer) 29
Trader 5, 27, 83

Tulip 27, 83
Turrethill (steamer) 112
UB 56 (submarine) 113
UC 47 (submarine) 113
UC 61 (submarine) 113
Union 83, 84
Union Packet 84
Union T. 84, 93
United 84
Vanquisher 84, 85
Verona (yacht) 116
Victoria 85
Warkworth 85
Warkworth (steamer) 93,110
Warkworth Castle 85, 85

Warkworth Harbour (steamer) 111
Waterwitch 15
Wave 86
Wave Spirit 13, 86
Wee Tottie 86
Westmorland 43
Widdrington 86, 87
Widgeon 87, 88
Wild Rose 88, 89
William 89
William Ash 70
Winstead (steamer) 81
Zealous 89, 90
Zetus 90

General Index

Of the many "tall ships" which have visited the North-East Coast in recent years, the wood brig *Ciudad de Inca,* seen here leaving the Tyne on 11 September 1982, has most in common with the square-rigged ships of Aln and Coquet. She was built in 1858 at Badelona, near Barcelona, Spain, is 92·1 feet long and has a breadth of 24 feet. While the main skysail is something of a gimmick, those deep single topsails, with their double rows of reef points, are real enough.

(Author)